The
Silver
Screens
of Wirral

(A history of cinemas in Birkenhead and Bebington)

by

P.A. Carson and C.R. Garner

First published 1990 by Countyvise Limited, 1 & 3 Grove Road, Rock Ferry, Birkenhead, Wirral, Merseyside L42 3XS, and Metropolitan Borough of Wirral, Central Library, Borough Road, Birkenhead, Wirral L41 2XB.

Copyright P. A. Carson and C. R. Garner, 1989.

ISBN No. 0 907768 32 6. Countyvise Limited.
ISBN No. 0 904582 09 4. Metropolitan Borough of Wirral Central Library.

Acknowledgement

The authors are indebted to many people who kindly donated information or photographs for use in this book. Whilst somewhat invidious to single out individuals they wish to record their thanks to the following. Mrs. B. Anderson (Wallasey), Mr. C. Bell (now living in Chirk), Mr. B. Bird (Wallasey), Mr. C. Bolton (Wallasey), Mr. I. Boumphrey (Prenton), Mr. F. Broadbent (Wallasey), Mr. G. Bryant (Eastham), Mr. A. Clayton (Wallasey), Mr. P. Dougherty (Port Sunlight), Mr. A. Eyles (London), Mr. R. Foster (Little Sutton), Mr. G. Houghton (Ellesmere Port), Mr. W. Houghton (Wallasey), Mrs. C. Gillespie (Liverpool), Mr. F. Gordon (Bromborough), Mrs. J. Hockey (Wallasey), Mr. N. Jenkins (Wallasey), Mr. T. Johnson (Neston), Mr. G. W. Kirkham (Ellesmere Port), Mr. F. Lindstrom (Irby), Mr. H. McQueen (Wallasey), Mr. D. Mitchelson (Bebington), Mr. C. Morris (Hoylake), Mr. G. Parker (Rock Ferry), Mr. S. Rebecca (Wallasey), Mr. W. Saxton (Liverpool) and Mr. D. Young (Pensby). Apologies are given to those who, quite unintentionally, escape due mention.

Gratitude is also extended to the North West Film Archive (Manchester Polytechnic) who provided two prints and to Mr. G. Weedon of the Fairground Heritage Trust. The authors were also impressed with the courteous and constructive service of the staff at the Public Libraries in Birkenhead, Ellesmere Port and Wallasey which facilitated the collection of relevant information and photographic material and generally removed much of the tedium from the research. Warm thanks also go to the staff of Wallasey Town Planning Dept. and to the management of The Top Rank Social Club and of the EPIC, both in Ellesmere Port.

Finally, the authors thank their families without whose support the text would not have been completed. In particular P.A.C. thanks his Wife, Kathleen, and their two sons, Paul and Neil, for their invaluable assistance with much of the laborious research of local papers. Kathleen also prepared the first typescript.

Dedication

The book is dedicated to:—

—a younger generation who wonder about the silver screens of a by-gone age.

—those who remember the silver screens yet still wonder.

—our wives, who wonder about us.

PAC/CRG

Preface

For some, the silver screens of yesteryear are simply remembered with nostalgia: the uniformed staff, the sparkling chandeliers, glittering fountains and sweeping marble staircases provided for ordinary people a form of escapism from the humdrum routine of the real world to the fantasy life-style of the stars on screen. For local historians, however, it is a record both of how the region adapted to, and applied, the emerging technology of electricity, cinematography, sound recording and amplification etc to mass entertainment, and how it exploited the new architectural opportunities for example in creating a combination of comfort and illusions of grandeur. As such this knowledge represents a valuable contribution to the social history of the region and adds to our appreciation of the life-style of the times. Furthermore, if one considers life on the peninsula to be a microcosm of that in Britain in general, then the fortunes of the cinema business in Wirral represent not only an important chapter in our local history but undoubtedly they provide an insight into the cinema industry throughout Britain. This relationship is confirmed by comparing UK cinema attendances between 1900 and the present day, with the pattern of the cinema business in Wirral over the same time span. Thus the Figure alongside shows that the distribution pattern of cinemas in Wirral parallels the figures for annual attendances at cinemas nation-wide.

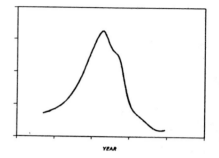

Trends in cinemas in Wirral

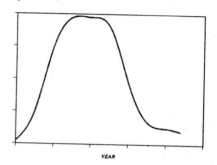

Attendances at UK cinemas

When it was eventually realised that the era of picture houses as they were known had passed for ever, some cinema buffs recaptured the magic of the period by building their own picture palaces such as the eleven-seater cinema built by one of the present authors on to his semi-detached house in Wallasey, and the twenty-six seat Whitegates precast cinema built by Keith and Jean Maxwell in Carr Lane. The former boasts a five foot screen equipped with silver satin curtain and a rainbow of lights. Mr. Garner has a wide collection of vintage "shorts" and full-length dramas backed up by filmed organ music and over 30,000 old "78" records. The Whitegates is a purpose-built cinema fitted out with plush wall-to-wall carpets, a shimmering screen, dimmer wall-lights and a cloakroom and toilets. Mr. Maxwell is currently projectionist in Ellesmere Port at the EPIC.

The aim of this book, however, is to provide a glimpse at the region's commercial silver screens of bygone days. These distinctive buildings of the 1920's and 1930's represent an important contribution to our heritage of 20th century architecture, in much the same way as did the railway stations of the 19th century. The main source of information was local newspapers augmented by personal memories of the authors and those of a host of colleagues. Whilst extensive records are available for many cinemas there is a dearth of data available for some of the older picture-houses since they tended to rely more on advertisements displayed in the local shops than in the press.

For convenience this book is published in two volumes. The other book is dedicated to the cinemas of the Wallasey region (Egremont, Liscard, Moreton, New Brighton, Seacombe and Wallasey) and the rest of the peninsular (Ellesmere Port, Heswall, Hoylake, Neston and West Kirby). This book describes cinemas of Bebington, Birkenhead, Claughton, New Ferry, Prenton, Rock Ferry and Tranmere. Each volume contains a general introduction, which is common to both, tables summarising seating capacity, opening and closing dates for the cinemas in chronological order, plus maps identifying their location. The cinemas are arranged throughout in alphabetical order.

Introduction

The dawn of an era

The birth of films clearly has its roots in the development of photography but the true history of motion pictures is more accurately linked with the Kinetoscope. This device, invented by Thomas Edison in 1889, consisted of a peephole cabinet inside which an illuminated length of film revolved on spools to project the image on the end of the cabinet. Usually the machines were coin operated and the films were about fifty feet in length and ran for less than a minute. The subjects of Edison's films were simple such as a dog with a bone, a baby being bathed, a boxing match, and so on, all chosen to show movement, albeit rather jerky. The first public showing of *projected* moving pictures took place on the roof of Madison Square Garden on May 20th 1895 and later the same year Louis and Auguste Lumiere of Lyons presented their first projection machine at the first public film show in Paris in December 1895. It was on February 20th 1896 that the first public projected film show was given in Britain. This was at the Regent Street Polytechnic (Marlborough Hall), London.

It is astonishing that the film industry developed so rapidly as a form of viable entertainment from such humble beginnings, and the first films were shown on Merseyside as early as November 1896 at the Argyle, Birkenhead. Indeed, this was claimed to be the first film show outside London but records suggest that films may have been screened earlier in the year at the St. James Theatre and the old Y.M.C.A., both in Manchester. Following the early innovation at the end of the nineteenth century, the cinema industry on Wirral developed in four distinct phases.

The first stage was at the turn of the century when 'animated picture shows' and 'bioscopes' were to be seen at fairgrounds. These tended to be a simple tent set up behind a highly decorative facade built around two bioscope wagons, turning the bioscope into one of the largest and most ornate shows in the fair. A typical example is depicted in the illustration on the following page. Pioneers included Pat Collins who ran cinemas in Walsall, the potteries and in New Brighton. During this initial phase films were somewhat of a experiment. Thus the first moving pictures seen by Wallaseyans were those shown at Pat Collins' "The Big Show" in the Palace covered amusement park on the promenade, New Brighton. One of the early films to be shown at these twopenny side shows around 1903 was *The Mad Barber* which depicted a man having a shave: when the razor suddenly slipped his head rolled to the ground and then commenced to dance around the picture sheet. At that time the shows were changed once a month and were operated by the Excelsior Company in conjunction with variety featuring two small singers and dancers known as *Tiny and Mite*. Collins' funfair later travelled to other parts of the peninsula and, for example, gave a Christmas show at Birkenhead Market Place in 1909 which, in addition to rides, animal acts and side shows, included all the latest and best animated pictures.

In parallel with the Bioscope, films began to be shown in public halls and later progressed to become a regular feature of music hall programmes. It was during this second phase of development that the cinema became a more serious form of entertainment. It is reported that moving pictures were shown at the YMCA in Grange Road, Birkenhead in the late 1890's and in 1899 animated film shows were given by a Mr. Vanderbilt (real name Roberts) on the other side of the Wirral at the Public Hall, West Kirby. By 1900 performances of Saronie's (Vanderbilt's brother) Gold Medal Cinematograph were given at the Town Hall, Hoylake and the Tynwald Hall, West Kirby. However, it was not until 1911 when Messrs. G. Fenton and V. Branford began presenting films at West Kirby's Public Hall (later the Queens cinema) that the first regular picture shows arrived in this part of the Wirral. Later the following year these gentlemen extended their activities to Hoylake when they took lease on the Hoylake Institute (later the YMCA). The first time that animated pictures were advertised as the main attraction at a public hall in Wallasey was in September 1904 at the Irving Theatre.

During this period the new phenomenon was pre-occupied with establishing respectability and the 'halls' initially aligned themselves with the accepted theatre as a form of entertainment, and they often continued to be called 'theatres' even when their programmes consisted mainly of animated films. In the early 1900's some Wirral variety theatres such as The Argyle, The Theatre Royal and The Hippodrome all in Birkenhead and the Irving, The Palace and The Tower Theatres, all in the Wallasey area, included films in their bill of fare. After their novelty value had been exploited some music halls reverted to live variety. Even then, however, some retained News Reels at the end of their

A typical bioscope

programmes as "chasers" to encourage all but the true film-lovers to leave, thereby assisting to empty the halls. The Institute in Neston, the Church Institute at Ellesmere Port and the Kings Hall in Heswall were all similarly used as places of entertainment.

By this time the early films, in addition to providing light entertainment, soon covered more serious subjects such as the funeral of King Edward VI and the subsequent coronation of King George V and Queen Mary. Despite the general acceptance by now of moving pictures as an established type of entertainment the art form was not without its critics. Issues debated with the arrival of the motion pictures included the potential deleterious effect of films on morals and on health, particularly with respect to eyesight. (To some extent this apprehension of a new and emerging technology can be compared with modern-day concern expressed about a host of potential hazards associated with use of visual display units). Despite concern expressed about standards it is interesting to note that in 1928 alone the local Justices examined almost one-thousand film synopses yet banned only one film.

The next phase in the advancement of the industry was the conversion of existing buildings such as billiards halls and unused chapels into "electric palaces" as exemplified by the Globe in Birkenhead and the Lyceum Electric Palace in Egremont both in 1910, and the Wallasey Picturedrome and the Electric Picture Palace in Rock Ferry both in 1911. The growing popularity of the movies also resulted in the conversion of music halls into picture-houses as exemplified by the Queen's Hall in Birkenhead and Tranmere Music Hall, Old Chester Road.

The trend in the 1920's for the creation of purpose-built Picturedromes and Super Cinemas represents the fourth stage in the development of the picture-house. Here the tendency was to design in (or at least claim) the luxury which had been a feature of the interiors of earlier theatre buildings. Even their description as "picture palaces" and the choice of aristocratic or exotic name reflected an attempt to market the industry with a grandiose image. However, not all cinemas lived up to proprietors' claims and the smell of disinfectant, liberal use of scent sprays and colloquial reference to the premises by patrons as "flea pits" seemed in conflict with the market image. During the next two decades the facilities increased in luxury and sophistication with the arrival of such establishments as the Ritz, Regal, Plaza and the Gaumont (both in Birkenhead and Wallasey), with their neon lights, pile carpets, bucket seats and mighty Wurlitzer and Compton organs.

The 'Talkies' arrived on the Wirral first in Wallasey in June 1929 at The Royal in Egremont and in Birkenhead at The Scala in August the same year. This heralded a rapid growth of the industry with attendances rising dramatically in the late 1920's and early 1930's peaking at its heyday between 1930 and 1950 with about thirty cinemas operating on the Wirral. The arrival of the talkies however also presented problems for many in the industry as illustrated by the demise of cinema orchestras. Within a year of the talkies the operators and proprietors of some sixty cinemas on Merseyside were locked in conflict. The operators complained of long hours of work and the nervous strain associated with long-running talkie pictures. In September 1930 the operators and electricians voted for strike action and the proprietors retaliated with threats of using university students to man the projection equipment. All-out strikes were averted, however, when a compromise was reached and the operators settled for improved conditions and money.

Although most picture-goers in the early days tended to frequent local cinemas, they gradually became less parochial in their taste, a trend aided by the improvements in public transport (eg. expanded bus services, the electrification in 1938 of the Birkenhead to New Brighton line) and the increasing popularity of the private motor car.

For a brief spell at the onset of the Second World War picture houses had to close by government decree. This ruling was soon rescinded and most cinemas re-opened on the 18th September 1939. In many cases, box-office takings were down during the war years, although some pictures continued to be well attended with "House Full" signs on display as cinemas provided a valuable means of relief from the worries and hardship during these troubled years. This was particularly noticeable in the outlying regions of the peninsula as exemplified by the Tudor at West Kirby, where attendances were boosted by the influx of evacuees into the district from the bomb targets of Birkenhead and Wallasey. During the War, over 300 British cinemas were destroyed by enemy bombs. The Wirral did not escape the ravages of enemy action and those cinemas badly damaged or completely destroyed included the Avenue, Palladium, Plaza and Ritz in Birkenhead, the Winter Gardens in New Brighton and the Cosmo (Coliseum) in Wallasey. It was also during this period that Sunday opening of cinemas was introduced for parts of Wirral, but only after much controversy and resistance from the Church, councillors and Licensing judges. Thus in 1943 licences were granted to the three local cinemas in Ellesmere Port to show films between 5.30 and 9.30 pm, except those of H category. For some parts of the Wirral Sunday opening came much later eg. 1949 in Bebington and 1962 in Neston.

Between 1945 and 1954 the region was caught between the end of the War and an economic boom when people throughout the land flocked to the cinemas in their millions. This was the era of Crosby, Hope and Lamour in the *Road to . . .* films, Mickey Rooney in the *Andy Hardy* series, Westerns by John Ford such as *Stage Coach* and *Fort Apache* and the Gangster movies as exemplified by *Angels with Dirty Faces* and *The Roaring Twenties*.

The Cinemas That Never Were

It is of interest to note that during the period of expansion more cinemas were planned for the region than were actually built. Thus in 1937 an application by Messrs. Pain and Blease was approved for a £40,000 luxury cinema and dance hall at the northwesterly junction of Teehey Lane and Village Road, Higher Bebington. Plans showed the seating capacity to be around 1200, with 393 in the balcony and 800 in the stalls. The dance hall would hold a further 270. The cinema never left the drawing board.

Also in Birkenhead, plans were approved before the war for the erection of a cinema in Woodchurch Road which was to be called either the Curzon or the Rex. This would have been the last cinema designed by Sidney Colwyn Foulkes for SM Super Cinemas Ltd. According to the plans the lower section of the auditorium marked a return to the traditional type of design. The upper walls and ceiling were to be completely plain. The outline of the proscenium would have closely followed that of the screen at either side of which were to have been two slender columns. The lighting was to have been by the Holophane Co. In addition to auditorium and stage lighting effects, the white surround at the back of what would now be termed a "floating screen" was to have been lit during the showing of a film with colour lighting synchronised to add atmosphere and effect to the picture. By September 1939 the foundations of the cinema had been laid on land near to the Half Way House but the outbreak of war brought an abrupt halt to all cinema constructions. Sadly the picture house was never completed but it was not until the middle of 1956 that the land was eventually sold for alternative use.

Artist impression of Regal (Wallasey).

Plans were approved by the Wallasey Council's Works Committee on Wednesday 14th July 1937 for a new super cinema to be built on the site of the Central Market in Wallasey Road. The £40,000 - £50,000 Regal was designed by the architects, Messrs. M.W. and W.M. Shennan of Hamilton Square, Birkenhead. The plans were for a cinema with seating capacity for 2,108, a cafe, balcony and its own car park. However this project was not pursued.

Likewise, the 30,000 residents of Bromborough were promised their own cinema in April 1930. Details for a 880 seater picture house were presented to the planners on behalf of Mr. F.G.B. Scaddy of 'Heathstone', Spital Road, Bromborough. The cinema was to be erected 70 yards from Bromborough Cross in Allport Lane on a site occupied by 'The Hollies' dwelling house. It was to be built in the Georgian style from rustic bricks and artificial stone dressing. Two small shops were to flank the main entrance. Inside, a stage and dressing room facilities were planned to enable small plays to be presented. The application was supported by Mr. A. Earnest Shennan of Liverpool, who emphasised the modern features which were embodied in the proposals, including the isolated operating suite to which access was gained only via a separate exterior entrance. Despite objections by Superintendent Ennion the proposal was approved but in the event Bromborough's cinema was never built. At the time of writing this book, plans were muted to build an entertainment complex in Bromborough housing a multi-screen unit, and so the 'village' may yet have its own cinema, albeit 60 years late!

The Cinema Organs

The arrival of the talkies heralded the end for orchestral accompaniment to the films and provided impetus for the cinema organists to display their talents as they became an integral part of new larger establishments. It is worthy of note that Birkenhead can claim to be the spiritual home of cinema organs since it was a Birkenhead man, Hope Jones, who first introduced electric action into organs in his workshop in Argyle Street. The Rialto in New Ferry and the Plaza, Regal and Ritz in Birkenhead all had Comptons (although after bomb damage the instrument at the Ritz was replaced by a Christie organ which had been reconditioned by Wurlitzer). Interestingly, there were more cinemas with organs in the Birkenhead area than elsewhere on the peninsula which tends to reflect the differences in age of the cinemas in the various parts of the region. Indeed, had the Regal been built, which had been planned for Wallasey in 1937, this would have been the first picture house in that part of the Wirral which had a theatre organ. The organ from the Regal, Birkenhead, was eventually transferred to the Winter Gardens in New Brighton.

Cinema organists became local and national celebrities in their own right, exemplified by Rowland Tims, Sydney Gustard, Lewis Oddie and Frank Gordon who were household names. Thus, Mr. Lewis Oddie, a Yorkshire man born in Brockhole became the local church organist at the age of twelve and had his first experience as a cinema organist when he went to America just before the First World War. Mr. Oddie was recruited to play the new organ in the Plaza in Birkenhead. This 3 manual/12 rank Compton, at the time, was the largest on Merseyside. Mr. Oddie was a regular radio broadcaster and a popular figure at the Plaza where he remained as resident organist until his untimely death in 1936. As a mark of respect the staff, commissionaires, attendants, page boys etc., in their blue and gold uniforms lined up outside the cinema as a guard of honour as Mr. Oddie's funeral cortege passed by. Mr. Frank Gordon became equally renowned as a local organist and radio broadcaster. Mr. Gordon, a Mancunian by birth, like Mr. Oddie began as a young church organist at fourteen years of age. Three years later he became resident pianist at Lewis', Manchester, by day and a ballroom danceband leader by night. In 1938 he succeeded Sydney Gustard, who had taken over duties from Mr. Oddie, as resident organist at the Plaza where he stayed until 1951, a period of employment broken only by his service with the Royal Navy in World War Two. In 1951 he moved to the Ritz where he played for a further six years during which time he was a regular radio broadcaster. At present Mr. Gordon lives in Ambleside Close, Bromborough and teaches organ students at his studio in Craines in Liverpool and is president of the Merseyside Organ Society. He still broadcasts and records for the BBC.

Sydney Gustard

Mr. Frank Gordon at the Christie Pipe Organ (Ritz) taken during a BBC recording session.

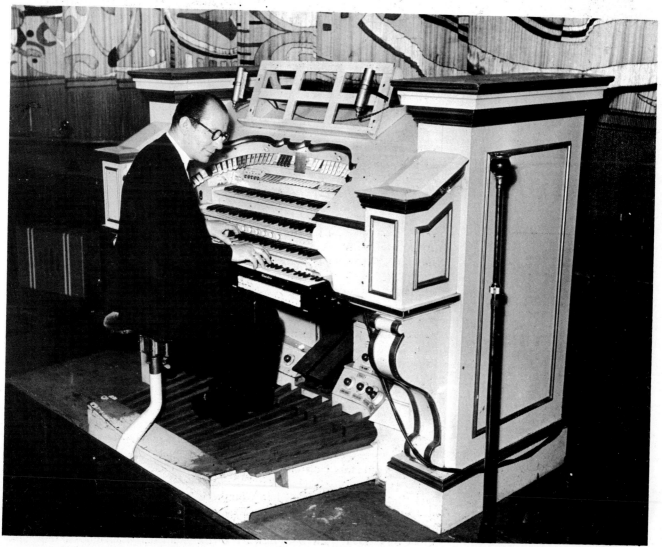

Henry Croudson and Lesley Walsh at the Regal (1939)

Mr. R. Saronie

The Impact of Cinema Owners and their Managers

Without a doubt the success of many picture-houses was directly attributable to the enterprise of their proprietors and management. As an illustration, James R. Saronie (real name Roberts), a Liverpool photographer and entrepeneur, began recording events of interest on film around Merseyside. His first films were just thirty feet long and took but a minute to screen. After some success with showing films at the YMCA and in halls across the peninsula, Mr. Saronie converted The Tranmere Music Hall, Old Chester Road, into the Coliseum (Picture Palace) in the first decade of the century. He went on to open the Electric Palace (later the Park Picture Hall) in Birkenhead and later the Scala at Prestatyn in North Wales where he made his home. The successful circuit, Bedford Cinemas Ltd., which owned many cinemas in the region at some stage of their life including the Lyceum (Egremont), Marina (New Brighton), Plaza (Birkenhead) and Trocadero (New Brighton), was created by Mr. J.F. Wood, who started in the early 1900's by renting the Queens Hall in Birkenhead and the Walton Baths Liverpool, for showing films. The venture proved so successful that by the end of that year he had built Liverpool's first purpose-built picture house, the Bedford Hall, Walton. Mr. Southan Morris started the SM chain whose aquisitions included the Kings (Heswall), Lyceum (New Ferry), Moreton Picture House, Neston New Cinema, Palladium and Picturedrome (both in Birkenhead), Queens (Ellesmere Port), Regal, Rio and Ritz (all in Birkenhead) and the Winter Gardens (both in Hoylake and in New Brighton).

The Gaumont - British Picture Corporation (formed in 1927 by Colonel A.C. Bromhead, Isidore Ostrer, C.M. Woolf, Michael Balcon and Lord Beaverbrook) owned the largest number of cinemas in Wirral, many of which formerly belonged to the Bedford chain.

Bill Boht at the Ritz Holiday Girl Contest (1950's)

Managers in the industry often came and went but a few, such as Bill Boht and Dick Rutherford dedicated their lives to the cinema business on the Wirral. Thus, Bill Boht from Liverpool started his career as a musician in cinema orchestras and soon progressed to musical director and then supervisor. With the arrival of the 'talkies' when the demand for cinema musicians disappeared he moved into administration becoming assistant manager in Preston. Following a brief spell there he moved to spend the major part of his career in Birkenhead, first at the Park Cinema followed by periods at the Super, Empire and then the Ritz as general manager, where, between 1937 and 1966, he stayed with the exception of his period in the Services as a Sergeant Major. The reputation of this cinema as the 'show place of the north' can be directly attributable in part to the endeavours of Mr. Boht and he soon established himself as a popular local figure. (In 1966 he moved to the Midlands to take control of administration of the Malvern Festival.) On the other side of the peninsula, Dick Rutherford had an equally distinguished life in the business. He joined in 1906 as a programme boy for the Adeler and Sutton's Pierrots at the Pier Pavilion, New Brighton. After leaving Wallasey Council School in 1911 he took a job at Wallasey's first cinema, The Palace, New Brighton. He became one of the first projectionists and joined Wirral Picturedromes Ltd, (Queens Picture House circuit) in 1913 with whom he remained for the rest of his working life becoming general manager of cinemas on both sides of the Mersey.

Dick Rutherford

An Industry in Decline

The late 1950's and the 1960's saw a dramatic decline in the UK cinema business: 1,640 million visits to cinemas were recorded in 1946 and only 70 million in 1986. In 1943 70% of the country's population had attended the cinema at least once between the months of June and July whereas in 1986 68% of the adult population never went to the cinema. The quality of the pictures and the sound, together with the standard of audience-comfort increased at an

13

exponential rate as did the general expectations of cinemagoers: ironically both were responsible for the initial success and for the subsequent decline of the cinema. More direct causes were attributed to rising costs (for example — of heating oil, wages, taxes) and the arrival of alternative forms of entertainment such as television and, more recently, video recorders. A major decline coincided with the introduction of BBC Television and a second followed the arrival of commercial television. Rows and rows of empty seats told their tale and cinemas were up for sale. Ambitious attempts were made by some managers to halt or even reverse the decline. This included introduction of extra-wide screen systems, 3-D, Cinerama, Tod-AO, Stereophonic Sound, late night performances and multi-unit houses. Any influence on the trend was temporary and the cinemas continued to close. Today the only silver screens operating in Wirral are Unit 4 in Wallasey, The Cannon in Birkenhead and Hoylake, and the Charles Haywood cinema at the EPIC in Ellesmere Port. In short, within a brief spell of about three quarters of a century, the Wirral experienced a rapid rise and equally-dramatic decline in the cinema as a means of mass entertainment.

This book charts for posterity the history of the individual cinemas that have existed on the peninsula from their inception at the end of the nineteenth century to the present day. Each possessed its own culture and style. They ranged in size from the tiny houses such as the 200 seater Wallasey Picturedrome to the large 3,000 seater Tower Theatre at New Brighton and the more modern dream palaces such as the Plaza in Birkenhead with a capacity of 2,500. The style of the auditoriums was as varied as the external architecture, many comprising single storeys whilst others boasted balconies which themselves ranged in size from the two tiny twelve-seater balconies at the Kings in Ellesmere Port to the huge circle at the Savoy which, with 768 seats, was larger than most cinemas in the region.

Cinemas of Bebington, Birkenhead, Claughton, New Ferry, Prenton, Rock Ferry and Tranmere

TABLE OF CINEMAS IN CHRONOLOGICAL ORDER OF OPENING

Date of Opening*	Date of Closing	Map Ref	Cinema	Seating Capacity	Architect
1862(1908)	1949	5	Queen's Hall Theatre	1300	—
1862(1911)	1956	8	Claughton Music Hall (later the Astor)	800	—
1864(1910)	1937	6	Theatre Royal (later the Scala)	1850	L. Hornblower
1868(1896)	1940	1	Argyle Music Hall	800	—
1879(1910)	1962	15	Coliseum	1200	—
1888(1930)	1934	7	Hippodrome (previously Ohmy's Circus then the Metropole)	1375	—
1897(1911)	1956	18	Palace (Rock Ferry)	600	—
— (1910)	1917	17	Electric Palace (Globe)	—	—
1911	1937	10	Saronies Electric Palace (later the Park)	1000	—
1911	1956	9	Picturedrome (later Roxy)	550	Campbell & Fairhurst
1912	1946	11	Price Street Picturedrome (later the Lyric)	900	—
1913	1962	19	Lyceum	1176	Nagington & Shennan
1913	1941	13	Palladium/Rio	800	Nagington & Shennan
1916	1956	4	Picture House (later the Super)	730	T.T. Reece
1917	present	3	Empire	800	A. Shennan
1923	1956	16	Regent	1100	—
1928	1941	14	Avenue	1200	—
1930	1973	12	Plaza	2500	A. Shennan
1933	1961	20	Rialto	1275	—
1937	1972	2	Ritz	2000	R. Crombie
1938	1982	6	Savoy	2000	—
1938	1970	21	Regal	1316	S.C. Foulkes
1938	1964	10	Gaumont	1700	W.E. Trent
1944	1957	13	Rio	600	—

* The date quoted refers to the opening of the building. The figure in brackets refers to the date films were first shown if this was different to the opening date.

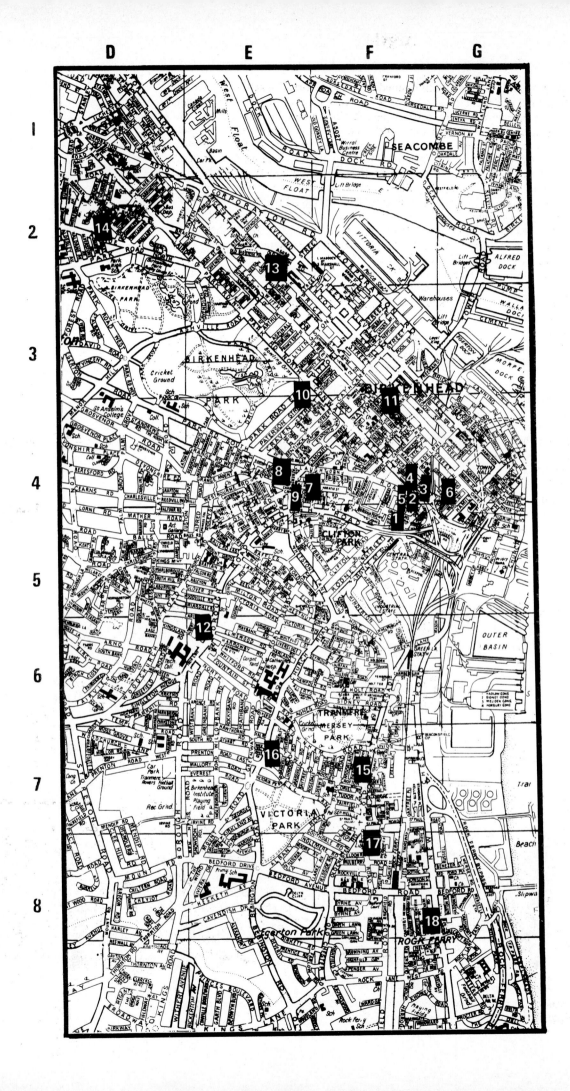

Argyle

The £10,000 Argyle Music Hall opened in Argyle Street, Birkenhead on 28th December, 1868 under the ownership of Mr. Dennis Grannel. It was a small buff brick theatre measuring only seventy feet by forty five feet with a seating capacity of around 800 comprising tables and chairs. Characteristic features included its tower, glass canopy, the decorative panel at the entrance proclaiming Argyle Theatre of Varieties and, high up, the opening date. Inside, narrow galleries ran down either side to the stage and the auditorium was festooned with pillars. The name of the theatre was changed in 1876 to the Prince of Wales and for several years it was used to present plays. In 1888 the system of running two shows nightly was tried for the first time. When Mr. Denis J. Clarke (Grannel's nephew) took control of the theatre in 1890 he restored the name 'Argyle' and it reverted to Music Hall style programmes. Under his forty five years stewardship the Argyle became as well-known nationally as the London Palladium is today. It attracted most of the big stars of the era, including Charlie Chaplin, G.H. Elliot, W.C. Fields, George Formby, The Crazy Gang, Pat Kirkwood, Harry Lauder, Stan Laurel, Donald Peers, Vesta Tilley, Wee Georgie Wood and many others.

Throughout its existence this distinguished theatre broke many records by becoming the first music hall to go on the air, the only music hall to broadcast throughout the Commonwealth and the first to broadcast direct to the U.S.A., on a coast-to-coast link-up. However, of the many milestones associated with this famous theatre, the date of Monday 9th November 1896 represents a special place in history. It was on that day the Argyle became Wirral's first cinema with a presentation of Messrs. Chard and Company's Vitagraph Living Pictures billed as the 'Photo-Electric Sensation of the Age'. Indeed, this was claimed to be the first film performance outside London where the animated pictures had been launched the previous year. The installation of electric lights at the Argyle specially for the occasion was an additional attraction. By all accounts the event was extremely popular as gauged by the huge attendances and the rapturous reports in the local press that week, as illustrated over page.

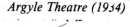

Argyle Theatre (1934)

The Liverpool Express reported — "The subjects selected for the pictures are very attractive and admirably adapted for proving the wonderful facility with which pleasing and familiar scenes can be effectively reproduced by the aid of the invention, several of the pictures are immensely amusing and the exhibition was enthusiastically applauded by a crowded audience."

The Birkenhead News said — "It has not infrequently been our task to give expression to feelings of pleasure at the high class, refined and exceptionally entertaining programmes presented by Mr. D. Clarke to the numerous patrons of the Argyle Theatre, but, perhaps, never in the annals of that favourite place of amusement has there ever been provided a more bright, attractive, and entertaining programme. One item on the bill is proving an immense attraction, and deservedly so. This is the Vitagraph, aptly described as the photo-electric sensation of the age. Those who have not yet had the privilege of seeing animated photographs will be thrusting away an opportunity of looking upon this scientific perfection if they fail to visit the Argyle this week. The scenes depicted, the exactitude with which they are carried through, and the clearness of the views are such as to call for unstinted praise, and it may be mentioned that in order to render the exhibition still more successful, an installation of electric light has been put into the building with the result anticipated."

The Birkenhead Advertiser claimed that — "The unusual attractions held out to his patrons by Manager Mr. Clarke, drew to his cosy hall on Monday and last evening's audiences that filled the building from floor to roof. The latest London attraction produced this week is the Vitagraph, a wonderful machine, which exhibits moving pictures and animated scenes from life, and depicts with extreme accuracy every day events as seen in our country and town life. To enable the pictures to be shown with greater effect, the management have installed the electric light, and without seeing the Vitagraph it is difficult to imagine the realism with which a storm at sea, boys fighting for pennies under the pier, children paddling on the beach, donkey riding, Brighton on Bank Holiday, are depicted."

The film show was supplemented with live entertainment including Mr. Pat Rafferty, the renowned Irish comedian. Admission charges were £1 1s and 10s 6d for Private Boxes, 2s 6d Single Seats, 1s 6d Circle, 1s Stalls and Balcony, Pit 6d and Gallery 3d. Reduced prices were charged after 9pm eg. Circle 1s, Balcony 6d but seats could not be guaranteed and readmission was not permitted. Performances started prompt at 7.30 but patrons could enter at 6.30 for an extra 6d. The following week's film programme included *The Czar in Paris, Gatwicks Paddock, Naval Gun Drill, Teasing the Gardener in Birkenhead Park, The Policeman and Cook, Bonfire Scene, Railway Train Arriving at Woodside Station,* and *March Past of Artillery at Aldershot,*

The Argyle continued to show films for a brief period in an attempt to attract patronage and to counter competition from its rival, the Gaiety Music Hall (later taken over by Denis J. Clarke). Examples included living pictures of the Corbett and Fitzsimmons fight in 1897. The full length film of the fight was billed as "The Sensation of the Season" displaying "every movement of the combatants, and the crowd, without any of the demoralizing surroundings unavoidable at the actual fight". Admission was between 3d and 2s 6d for single seats with boxes advertised at between 10s 6d and a guinea. Even though the Argyle reverted to live entertainment as its main bill of fare, they retained News Reels as regular features to end their programme.

In the Summer of 1909 the Argyle underwent six weeks of refurbishment and re-opened on Monday 20th September of that year. The most notable alteration was the new entrance to the stalls and boxes, which, as well as providing a most elegant adjunct to the theatre, also functioned as an emergency exit. It was situated on an angle at the corner of Argyle Street and Oliver Street and had been constructed by taking in the shop premises which had formerly occupied one corner of the block. The entrance led into an octagonal vestibule, decorated with Corinthian columns, panelled dome ceiling, marble steps, and ornamental terrazzo paving. A pair of mahogany doors led from the vestibule into the waiting hall, the ceiling and walls of which were panelled in plaster; the floor was covered with crimson carpet and the fittings were of mahogany. The staircase from the hall was in Sicilian marble with ornamental handrails on either side and in the centre. The lounge for those occupying the stalls and boxes had also been rearranged and greatly enhanced. The prevailing colours of the decorative

scheme were gold and cream which, together with the mahogany timberwork, gave a rich appearance. The leaded lights to the windows and the electric light fittings created additional artistic finishes, whilst the new cloakrooms and toilets provided important functional improvements as did the installation of two powerful electric fans to increase ventilation. The theatre had been decorated throughout and greatly upgraded by re-seating in the stalls, dress circle and pit, and the carpeting of the stalls. The private boxes had also been completely refurbished, carpeted and fitted with plush draperies. The new pay box was open between 10am and 4pm and again in the evening. The modifications were carried out by Mr. T. Taliesin who made ingenious use of space and the final effect was to convert the Argyle into one of the 'cosiest theatres in the country'.

The re-opening programme comprised Victoria Monks (vocalist and impersonator), Mooney and Holbein (a vaudeville turn) together with other stage performances. This trend for live entertainment continued although, like the Theatre Royal, the Argyle was showing films of the funeral of the late King Edward VII in 1910 and in 1911 pictures of the coronation of King George and Queen Mary. Interestingly, it would seem that the electricity supply installed for the first film show in November 1896 was somewhat of a temporary arrangement since later reports described how special cables had to be "set up" along the streets to the Argyle in order to power the projectors because the theatre was not equipped with its own supply of electricity.

The Argyle was refurbished again in 1913 with a novel lighting system comprising heavily mounted brass torches and flambeaux. The new decor in the auditorium included a copy of the Parthenon Frieze at the British Museum and was arranged by W. Scott Morton. The subjects comprised in the frieze were from each group represented in the original frieze. The incident of the

Argyle Theatre (1926)

Argyle bomb damage (1940)

presentation of the peplos between the two groups of deities was the central feature of the whole composition; to the left of these groups was a procession of virgins bearing sacrificial vessels approaching magistrates. To the right of these deities and magistrates there was a second group of virgins also carrying vessels. Following these were cows and sheep for sacrifice with attendants, bearers of fruit, musicians, sages, charioteers and horsemen, and youths carrying bottles. The festival depicted represented the Panathenaic procession to the ancient temple of Athene Polias on the acropolis. It was of both religious and political significance and represented all that was best of youth, beauty, nobleness and honour in Greece. The gods and godesses were in an easy sitting posture as if waiting for the arrival of the procession and the presentation of the sacrifices and offerings. The seated attitude gave the sculpture the opportunity to represent them in greater size that the mortals in other parts of the freize. The seats which were being carried by two females were supposed to be for the priest and priestess after the delivering of the peplos.

Mr. Sam Austin, who lived at 21 Holly Grove, Tranmere, recalled the early days at the Argyle, when the patrons sat around drinking ale during the entertainment and how the proceedings were conducted by the old style chairman under extremely strict conditions. Indeed, records reveal how artistes were fined for a late arrival. Mr. Austin was stage-doorman at the Argyle in the 1920's during which time he was beseiged by hundreds of autograph hunters attempting to get back stage for coveted signatures. He dealt out hundreds of different excuses to the fans but exploited the opportunity himself, collecting some three hundred autographs by 1930!

Following the death of Denis J. Clarke in 1934 his son took control.

On 21st September 1940 the Argyle suffered a direct hit in one of the worst bombing raids on Birkenhead during the war. Following the collapse of the roof the building was virtually reduced to ruins; only the outer facade remained with just sufficient of the building to use as a store for theatrical costumes for a period in the 1960's. Despite several proposals as late as 1956 to rebuild the theatre the schemes never materialised because of the costs (estimated at £110,000) and the discouraging post-war experiences with provincial variety halls. The site was eventually cleared for use as a car park for customers of Beatties department store.

Argyle Theatre – exterior plaque

Argyle Theatre up for sale

Avenue (circa 1930)

Avenue Super Cinema

The Avenue Super Cinema Co. Ltd., with an authorised capital of £30,000 had been set up to control the building of the 1200 seater red-brick cinema at the junction of Bidston Avenue and Norman Street. It was officially opened on 2nd February 1928 by the Mayor, Alderman F. Naylor. Mr R.H.F. Hindle, Chairman of the Board of Directors, welcomed the Mayor and paid tribute to the quality of workmanship by the men from Birkenhead who had laboured on the project which had negated the need to use outside contractors. Apologies were made for the unfinished state of the premises with promises that the cinema and the cafe would be completed within two weeks. The Mayor expressed how impressed he was with the outcome, his only regret being that it had not been sited in Tranmere. He went on to make great play of the poor quality of films often being screened in the area but he was confident that the proprietors of the Avenue Super Cinema would ensure that only a high standard of family entertainment would be provided at the town's newest picture-house.

The cinema, which was constructed by Messrs. John Evans Ltd., embodied all the latest features and was considered ahead of its time in design. The building, 165 feet in length and 18 feet wide at the front fanning out to 100 feet at the rear was, on either side, fronted by its own car park illuminated by roof mounted floodlights. A tall flagpole was also mounted on the roof-top. Two imposing entrances featured marbled plateaux and archways with 15 cwt keystones. The two main entrances, each with their own pay boxes, were floodlit and above, the cinema's name was illuminated by 166 flashing red and white lamps. Access to the cheaper seats could also be gained via pay boxes at the narrower end of the building. The external illuminations had been undertaken by W.H. Trace and Sons, a local electrical concern.

Inside the Avenue (1928)

The handsome main foyer was spacious, fully carpeted and magnificently adorned with Austrian oak doors and with noble colonnades rearing to a lofty ceiling. Teak tread stairways either side of the foyer led to an upstairs cafe and the 422 seater balcony via an elegantly tiled mezzanine lounge where second house patrons could wait rather than queue outside.

The unique fan shape of the pillarless auditorium provided a spacious seating arrangement with sumptuously upholstered lift-up seats in rows of 22 at the front and 40 at the rear. The 33½ feet high ceiling was elegantly moulded and the orange coloured walls displayed blue dado panelling with frames of Austrian Oak. The Holophane duo-phantom interior lighting, incorporated in the decorative features on the ceiling, was a particularly novel feature. This was installed by the Etna Lighting and Heating Co. Ltd., of Birmingham and was designed by the Welshman, Mr. E. Gillespie Williams who was present at the opening ceremony. By clever application of a ceiling-mounted prism and floodlight system the interior was illuminated with a constantly changing array of over one thousand different colour combinations and causing the central sun feature on the curtains to go through the process of dawn, noon, sunset and nightfall. The carpets, foyer furniture and curtains had been supplied by Messrs. Charles Taylor (Liverpool) Ltd.

The spacious stage hid dressing rooms and a managers office. The building was air conditioned using extract ventilation to remove foul air and a system to wash the incoming fresh air. The plenum system provided 550 cubic feet of air per hour. Heat was generated by two powerful Robin Hood boilers rather than the more common stoke hole. The operating room, the cinema's nerve centre, was of fire-proof design.

The 7.30 pm opening programme consisted of a performance by Roland Jackson and the Avenue Grand Orchestra under the direction of Mr. Andrew C. Bowden, the well-known cellist. Films shown were the latest Pathe Gazette, *The Toreador's Return* starring Charlie Chaplin and *Convoy* one of the best sea pictures of the day.

In the main the staff who all wore uniforms provided by the management, remained with the Avenue from the time it opened until its untimely closure. Amongst them were Miss Hosker (manageress), Mr. Jones (the commissionaire — a tall, slim man of military bearing with a small moustache), Miss I. Harris (cashier at the Bidston Avenue entrance), Miss E, Fenton (of the cafe who became Mrs. Dixie Dean), Miss O. Atkinson, Miss Jennion, Miss Iddon, Miss Horton, Miss "Buth" Mercer, Fred Williams and Mr. Kirk (a uniformed fireman/handyman). Prices of admission ranged from 6d and 1/- in the stalls to 1s 6d and 2s 4d in the balcony and all proceeds of the opening performances were devoted to local hospitals.

The talkie premiere at the Avenue, *The Desert Song* starring John Boles, was on August Bank Holiday Monday 1930.

Unfortunately, the Avenue had a brief life being a casualty of the blitz on 12th March 1941 when Merseyside suffered one of its worst bombing raids. Throughout its short existence of thirteen years, this cinema proved to be one of Birkenhead's most popular dream palaces. War damage, particularly to the foundations at the Norman Street end of the cinema however, left the ruins irrepairable and unsafe and, as a consequence, they were eventually demolished and the site was cleared for The Avenue public house to be erected.

Staff outing to Blackpool (1929)

Miss Mercer and Miss Harris

Miss Harris and other staff

Miss Atkinson and other staff

23

Claughton

The Claughton Music Hall, which opened in January 1862 in Birkenhead, stood at 271—273 Claughton Road on the corner of Atherton Street. It was the first of the town's five main music halls and was known originally as the 'Birkenhead Music Hall' but was soon more commonly referred to as the 'Claughton Music Hall' to avoid confusion with the other halls that opened later in the town.

The exterior of the building was lavishly decorated with ornate panels and medallions. Queen Victoria looked down over the main entrance on the North front whilst the faces of Weber, Handel, Beethoven, Haydn and Mendelssohn were carved in sandstone high on the East wall.

The interior consisted of two halls, the main one seating 600 and the smaller hall seating 200. Also, below the main auditorium were a small ballroom and ancillary rooms.

The "Hall" was opened with a celebration ball on Wednesday 16th January 1862 and amongst the 400-450 present was Mr. John Laird MP. The Hall lights emphasized the superior taste both in terms of the function and in the design of the fittings. Tickets for the grand event at 10/6 each were somewhat expensive for the day. From then on the Hall was used for amateur dramatics by, amongst others, members of the 2nd Cheshire Rifle Volunteers commencing with Tom Taylor's comedy *Still Waters Run Deep*. Admission cost 3/- or 4/- and performances generally commenced at 7.30, although the doors opened at 7pm. In addition to theatrical events the Music Hall was also used for bazaars, jumble sales and the like. One notable function was in 1891 when a "grand Bazaar" was held in aid of the new Sunday school for St. Catherine's, Tranmere. This was under the patronage of Her Grace, the Duchess of Westminster. A few years earlier in 1877 the first council meeting of the newly incorporated 'Borough of Birkenhead' took place in the Claughton; this was in the days before the Town Hall was built.

In 1882 an organ was erected by Messrs. W. & F. Hall in the main hall to accompany oratorio performances. About 1892 the building was reputedly purchased by the Freemasons but still continued as a music hall. Famous personalities appearing at the Claughton included Sir Charles Halle, Clara Butt and Jerome K. Jerome.

The Music Hall moved into the era of "electric moving pictures" when it closed in 1911 for conversion into a cinema. (Around this time a public house opened nearby and was called the Music Hall in an attempt to perpetuate the name in the area; the public house survived until the early 1970's). The new premises, which had been tastefully re-decorated, opened on 1st April 1912 as a high class picture palace under the management of Messrs. Alfred Moscow and Louis Baxter who also led the Casino Orchestra. The opening performance began with a rendition by the orchestra of Wagner's grand March *Tannhauser*. The remainder of the programme consisted of films interspersed with orchestral pieces and solo performances by Miss Mabel Hamer. The films commenced with *The Author's Conquest*, a comedy which centred around a successful author whose approaches by unknown admirers leads to misunderstandings by his wife, but which concluded satisfactorily. Other films included *Rogan (France) and its Environs*, a beautiful scenic travelogue; *Norma from Norway* and *One Touch of Nature* both dramas; *The Girl in the Cab* a comedy, and ending with the tragedy, *The Half-Breed's Daughter*. Admission was at 1/- and 6d. The large crowds showed their appreciation with raptuous applause for the films, artistes and the orchestra, and their continued support over the following weeks was a testimony to the success of this cosy cinema. By May of that year the Claughton Picture House was announcing that the house was under new management, but it seems that this was associated with the changes resulting from the recent re-opening.

In 1913 the Claughton Picture Palace reopened after a short period of closure with Mr. Temperley as the acting manager and performances were twice nightly with entrance at 3d, 6d, 9d and 1/-. Matinee performances were on Mondays, Thursdays and Saturdays at 3pm. The opening programme included a mixture of comedies which were "free from vulgarity yet capable of creating roars of applause", plus an educational film. On Thursday afternoons the films were supplemented by cello solos.

British Thomson-Houston sound equipment was installed in 1930 and on 16th June that year the first talkie screened at the Claughton was *Sunny Side Up*, a superb singing and dancing musical with Janet Gaynor and Charles Farrell.

*Claughton Picture House
(1970's)*

In September 1952 the cinema was taken over by the Woodhill Entertainment Company Ltd. of Manchester and after redecoration and the installation of new seats 'and sound equipment it re-opened as the Astor cinema with Mr. C. Simmons continuing as manager. It has been suggested that the new name for the cinema stemmed from John Jacob Astor (1763-1848), the founder of the Astor family of American millionaires.

A deliberate change in management policy was announced in 1956 when the Astor was closed for redecoration and refurbishing before reopening one week later as the town's first Continental picture-house. Mr. C. Simmonds, the manager for the previous eighteen months, continued in the post. Alas, this attempt to fight the trend of closures by providing specialist films for a select segment of the market failed and, when the proprietors decided not to renew the lease, the Astor closed a few months later with a performance of *Fire in the Skin* plus *Five Boys from Barska Street*.

The cinema portion of the property was offered at auction whilst the adjoining Empress Ballroom tenancy continued for a further twelve months. Subsequent applications to transform the building into various ventures failed. In 1957 the premises were acquired by Mr. Harry Rogers who converted it into the Town's first Bingo Hall. This opened in 1958 as The Charing Cross Social Club and the Astor Tombola Club. Although the Club was popular for many years with the 900 seats usually fully occupied, it closed early in 1981 and, after the fixtures were sold, the premises with its 12,000 square feet of floor space were put on the market. All attempts to find a buyer floundered and the fabric of the building, which by then was over a century old, had deteriorated during its last two decades to such an extent that it became structurally unsound. The harsh winter of 1981/82 took its final toll and, because of the dangerous state of the derelict building, it was demolished in March 1982.

Coliseum

(Tranmere Music Hall)

The premises at 218 Old Chester Road, Tranmere, erected by Mr. J.M. Harrison as a Music Hall and Assembly Rooms, opened on the evening of Saturday 15th November, 1879. The inaugural concert was given by Liverpool Vocalists' Union conducted by Mr. T. Jones with Miss Harriet Leders, Miss Clara Nicholl and Mr. B.B. Pierpoint; Mr. W.I. Argent accompanied the singers and gave two solo performances on the harmonium. The hall was rather large with capacity to accommodate 1200 people, and its structure was considered to be especially convenient for its intended use. For nigh on a quarter of a century the Hall was let for political and public meetings, Sunday School anniversary services for the small Congregational Mission Hall in nearby Randle Street, and mainly for theatrical performances. It was adapted for showing films in the first decade of the present century by the local entrepreneur James R. Saronie, when it then became known as Saronie's Coliseum (and later disparagingly referred to by patrons as the "flea pit"). The original programmes consisted of a mixture of film shows and live variety. Typical of the early shows at the Coliseum were films of local events taken by the proprietor himself (a professional photographer with studios in Liverpool) and shown on the 'bioscope', coupled with live performances ranging from animal acts such as performing ponies and a dog circus, to interludes of local turns — a form of talent spotting. If the audience disapproved of an act they left management in no doubt of their opinions and Mr. Saronie became expert in judging his patrons' mood, throwing the building into darkness before the audience became hostile and the missiles began to fly.

Whilst many early Wirral cinemas developed children's matinees, none were more popular than the 'Penny Rush' on Saturday afternoons at the Coliseum when the entering audiences dropped their penny admissions into a fire bucket under the watchful eye of the management.

Since there were limited copies of the films (indeed often only the one) the practice at the end of each performance was to dispatch the film by bicycle to the next cinema for showing. In the not-unusual event of the arrival of the film being delayed the audience obligingly filled in the time with community singing.

Tranmere Music Hall (tall building on left, next to shops)

There was always an element of rivalry between the nearby Electric Palace and the Coliseum, the former being considered somewhat superior to the latter by locals in Rock Ferry, a view not supported by Tranmerites.

In October 1928 a fire resulting from faulty electrics, broke out in the film rewind room during a childrens matinee. The manager, Mr. Cecil D. Lindsay immediately took up a position at the front of the balcony and ordered the pianist to strike up a medley of popular airs and the children were marched singing from the building unaware of the emergency. Fortunately, the fire had been extinguished by the time the fire brigade had arrived, and within twenty minutes of the start of the incident the programme had recommenced. By strange coincidence the following week the film advertised on the posters outside the picture house was aptly entitled *Fireman, Save My Child*. (Although the fire proved not to be serious, the wisdom of the manager's quick action was confirmed by the horrific outcome of another picture house fire just fourteen months later. This occurred in Scotland where seventy children lost their lives in a frantic scramble for the exit following the outbreak of fire at the Glen Cinema in Paisley on New Years Day, 1930. The Mayor of Birkenhead sent a telegram to Paisley in sympathy.)

March past of Brownies

After World War I the Coliseum was taken over by the precursors of Cheshire Picture Halls Ltd., with Mr. William F. Williams as manager. The date of the first talkie is uncertain because this cinema was not advertising on a regular basis in the local press in 1929. However it seems likely that talkies became part of the programme at the end of October 1929, the first advertised talkie being *Weary River* starring Richard Barleness on 8th November and this attracted big crowds. Soon after Al Jolson featured in *The Singing Fool*. In the second quarter of the century the cinema passed into the hands of S.M. Super Cinemas.

In March 1958 the Coliseum again narrowly escaped serious damage by fire. Fortunately, a police man on the beat in the early hours detected smoke and on investigating discovered many of the seats ablaze in the smoke-filled auditorium. As a result of his action only carpeting and seats were affected. As with fires at many cinemas, the cause on this occasion was suspected to be a smouldering cigarette.

Also that year the cinema suffered a spate of what first appeared to be petty theft. Upon more detailed investigation however, the total loss amounted to almost £2,000 and the culprit proved to be the cinema manager himself who had taken his employer's money to pay off gambling debts

By the mid fifties the Coliseum became part of the Essoldo conglomerate who reluctantly announced the closure of the towns oldest remaining cinema in 1962 with the possibility of converting it into a bingo hall. However, this alternative option failed to transpire and the property was put on the market. The empty building stood derelict for some years before being acquired in the mid 1960's by Saunders Bros. who converted it into a furniture store which trades to this day. The last advertised film was "A Story of David" starring Jeff Chandler.

Coliseum (1920's)

Coliseum up for sale (1963)

Electric Palace
(Park Cinema)

James R. Saronie, owner of the Coliseum in Tranmere, spared no expense in the extensive alterations needed to convert the skating rink near Birkenhead Park Entrance into the Electric Palace cinema at 1a Park Road East. This was opened by the Mayoress, Mrs. Willmer, in February 1911 when she unveiled the statue of "Mercury" above the striking dome feature. This statue was intended to represent the light so necessary for the pictures. The entire proceeds from the grand opening were devoted to the Ship Yard lock-out fund and the programme included cinematographic films and a galaxy of variety talent.

This cinema was a low, single-storey building with a seating capacity of around 1,000. Seats were arranged on a raked floor raised some four feet at the rear of the auditorium, the best seats being of tip-up design and finished in blue plush. Attention was given to the emergency escape facilities such that the entire audience could evacuate in three minutes. The very "latest system of hot water heating apparatus" was installed to ensure the comfort of patrons. Projection equipment was a Silent Kaman machine in a projection booth measuring 6 feet by 2 feet 6 inches. In the early days as the Saronie Electric Palace the cinema boasted a small orchestra comprising a piano and strings. When the cinema changed hands and became the Park the new owners dispensed with the orchestra in favour of a 'Panatrope' which was simply an amplified gramophone.

The price of seats ranged from 2d to 1/- in the Grand Circle. Performances commenced at 8pm with 2.30 matinees on Saturdays when for 1d admission children were also given a barley sugar stick.

The Park had an uneventful existence and the last performance was on the night of 5th June 1937. This occasion was marked by the attendance of Councillor and Mrs. P.A. Allery, the deputy mayor and mayoress who recalled the twenty six year history of the cinema from the conversion of the skating rink to present times and announced that The Park Cinema was to be demolished to make way for an ultra modern super Gaumont cinema.

Electric Palace (circa 1911)

Electric Picture Palace
(Globe)

The Electric Picture Palace situated at 17 Grove Road, Rock Ferry opposite the public library opened to a full house on Monday 21st November 1910 at 7pm. The first films included an Indian Story, *The Way of the Red Man*, plus *Her Rival* and *The Rosary*. The hall, which hitherto had been used as a billiard hall, was leased for a term from Lancashire and Cheshire Billiard Halls Ltd who had removed their tables. The lessees, Messrs. Dawson, Fletcher and Starkey, had converted the premises into a cosy picture hall with the comfort of their patrons in mind. Plush seats of the tip-up variety were installed and entrance was at the popular price of 4d, 6d and 8d.

The policy of the management was to present whatever style of entertainment the public demanded. Because of the popularity of animated pictures the aim was to provide high class and up-to-date cinematographic entertainment coupled with live turns if so required. As a result early programmes included twice nightly performances of films at 7pm and 9pm with childrens matinees on Saturdays at 3pm. Amateur singing contests were featured on Thursdays at 9pm when special prizes were awarded. Films were changed twice each week and regular attractions included Fatty Arbuckle, a popular star of the times and Pearl White serials. It closed about seven years later (allegedly because the manager absconded with the weeks takings) before reverting to a billiard hall. The building stands to this day and is used as a factory making protective clothing.

The Globe building as it stands in 1989

Empire Picture Hall

(Classic/Cannon)

The Empire opened at 30/32 Conway Street, Birkenhead on 26th May, 1917. These erstwhile business premises were transformed into an up-to-date cinema by Messrs. Davies and Gaskell under the supervision of the well-known architect Mr. A.E. Shennan who had been responsible for the design of several similar edifices in the district. The main thrust of the design was to provide comfort for a relatively few patrons rather than mediocre facilities for many. This they achieved and the impression visitors experienced on crossing the threshold was one of 'lofty spaciousness'. The seating capacity of the ground floor was 600 whilst that of the small balcony was 200. A sloping floor ensured that all members of the audience had a clear view of the screen from any of the tip-up seats.

The interior decor was one of luxury consistent with war time economy: the entrance hall and stairs were of marble finished in dark oak panelling. Hanging lights in the hall and those up the stairs and in the lounge were "artistically arranged". The floors were lushly carpeted and the plasterwork was a feature throughout the building. As with many cinemas the ventilation was claimed to be so effective that in hot weather the temperature inside the picture house was cooler than outside. To compensate for inclement weather a heating system had also been installed.

With regards to entertainment, music was provided by Mr. Gus Savage and the opening film presented under the management of Mr. W.F. Armitage was *Storm and Sunshine. The Doctor's Secret* starring Miss Ruth Chatterton, Mr. H.B. Warner and Mr. John Loder, was the first 'talkie' to be shown at the Empire. This film was screened on 12th August 1929 thus making the Empire only the second cinema to introduce sound pictures to Birkenhead. The title of the film was considered more apt than 'Half an Hour', the book by Sir J.M. Barry upon which the film was based using as the plot a variation on the eternal triangle. Also included on the bill was a film of Mr. Ramsay MacDonald, the Prime Minister, speaking to the Nation from his home.

Conway Street (early 1900's)

Conway Street, Birkenhead

Empire (1946)

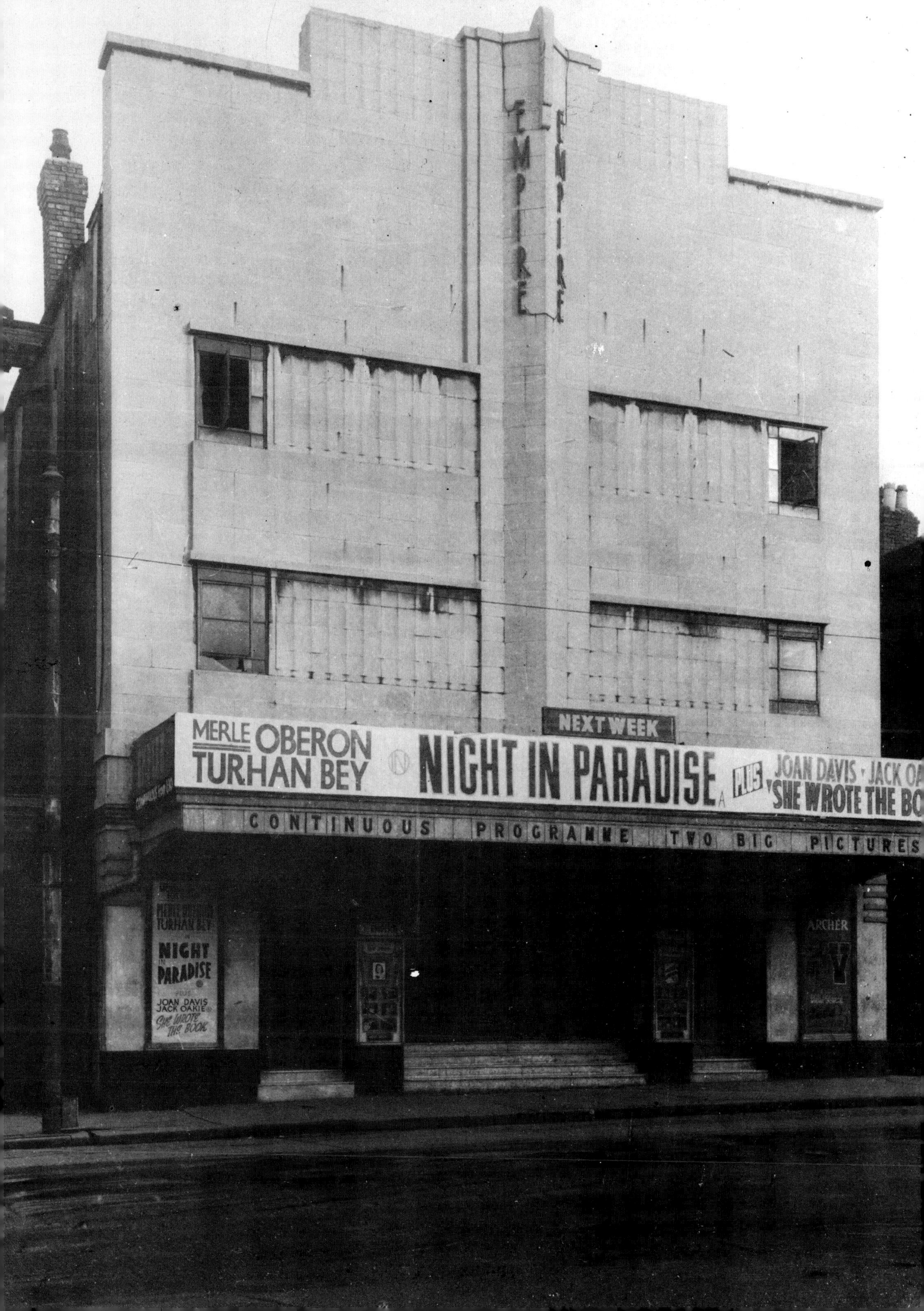

MERLE OBERON
TURHAN BEY

NIGHT IN PARADISE

NEXT WEEK

JOAN DAVIS · JACK OA
SHE WROTE THE BO

CONTINUOUS PROGRAMME TWO BIG PICTURES

Classic (1989)

An extensive modernisation programme in the mid 1930's resulted in refurbishment to both the interior and exterior of the theatre. These changes included a new lighting system which comprised concealed lights in the ceiling coves and around the proscenium surround as the sole source of illumination in the auditorium. The Empire operated as a bingo hall for a period during the 1960's but re-opened as the 'New Essoldo Luxury Cinema' on St. Valentines Day, 1969. With the advent of television and bingo in the 1950's the demand for large capacity cinemas had declined. Mr. Thomas Robertson, the Assistant Manager of the Essoldo Circuit Group, explained that the recent improvements to the old Empire were to reflect changes over the last ten years in audience expectations for a standard of luxury equivalent at least to the comforts of their own home; they would no longer tolerate uncomfortable cramped conditions with little leg room to watch films spoilt by many distractions. As a result almost 300 of the original seats had been removed leaving an even smaller balcony and only 314 in the reseated stalls. A new, wide screen was installed in front of the original proscenium which necessitated re-siting of the exit adjacent to the stage. Use of the concealed lighting system was discontinued and the theatre was lit only by floodlights from the front of the circle. Direct consequences of these refurbishments were for films to be shown for extended periods of four to six weeks to compensate for the reduced capacity, and an immediate increase in admission charges. An invited audience of civic leaders, heads of industry, commerce and social organisations were present at the re-opening to see Ross Hunter's *Thoroughly Modern Millie* and *The Magnificent Seven*.

Whilst it is dangerous to generalise this cinema developed a reputation for specialising for a time in horror movies in the 1960's. The picture house became the Classic in 1972 and more recently the Cannon. Currently it is the only commercial cinema in operation in Birkenhead, albeit now with just the stalls area in use.

Gaumont

Plans to rebuild the Park Cinema were presented to the magistrates on 21st January 1937, six months before the Park actually closed and it was estimated that it would cost around £40,000 to implement. The new cinema provided accommodation for 1,694 people with 1,128 on the ground floor and 326 in the balcony. This represented an increased capacity of 766 which would be achieved by increasing the hall area by 50% to 1400 square feet. Questions raised about the ventilation and the speed with which the building could be evacuated in an emergency (two minutes) were dealt with satisfactorily. However the magistrates took issue with the architect about the width of the exits, pointing out that those at the back of the circle were only four feet wide. In reply, the designer emphasised that regulations required three five-feet exits for over 250 visitors and that the plans showed two five-feet exits plus two four-feet doors which represented an excess escape capacity. Eventually the plans were approved subject to all exits being five foot in width.

The Gaumont cinema, Birkenhead, was eventually built at 1a Park Road East facing Birkenhead Park on the site previously occupied by the Park Cinema. The designer was W.E. Trent, assisted by D. Mackay of the Gaumont-British architects department. The main thrust of the design was in the modern idiom with emphasis on simplicity rather than ostentation: it was functional but preserved the quiet dignity of the residential district.

The main elevation was faced with a light faience at the base and above the main entrance while the flanking walls were finished in autumn-tinted bricks. The central facade was relieved by a series of five large windows and by three plaques representing Pierrot, Pierrette and Clown. A broad central canopy and two side canopies provided both added attraction and shelter for queuing patrons. The Gaumont name sign surmounted the central faience. At night architectural features were illuminated by neon- and flood-lights.

Gaumont (1938)

Gaumont (1938)

The principal features of the spacious entrance vestibule were the centrally-located pay box and kiosk, the polished Walnut joinery, the textured walls finished in coral pink with fluted frieze in fibrous plaster which concealed the lighting, and the Roman stone terrazzo flooring. Two staircases ascended to the circle lounge above the entrance hall. This was a large comfortably-appointed light and airy, luxurious room for waiting patrons. The five tall windows overlooking the park afforded a pleasant outlook, which was reflected in the cheery colour scheme of the lounge.

In the auditorium the magnificent ceiling, the proscenium and the sweeping lines of the side walls were highlighted only by relief and a tasteful colour scheme. The side walls were divided into sections comprising alternate vertical panels of blue and fawn, the latter hue forming the background for a series of abstract designs. The plain proscenium opening was flanked by coves indirectly illuminated and the ceiling above the arch swept outwards in a series of stepped coves which concealed the ceiling lighting. The illumination was provided by six large pendant fittings specially designed to flood the ceiling, whilst a continuous ring of light on the underside, coupled with illuminated metal fins, added to the artistic effect. The comprehensive stage lighting system comprised a 37 foot three-colour footlight with sixty three compartments; two 32 foot battens wired as footlights and fitted with three pilots; three 1,000 watt acting area lanterns, pattern 56, complete with gelatines and a switchboard and dimmer regulator fitted with "Sunset" dimmer. In total some 3,000 lamps were used in the direct and indirect lighting system. The main stage curtains were executed in pale blue velour with a broad silver band and deep fringe along the lower edge with matching pelmet, whilst the remaining stage draperies were in cream coloured satin with an appliquéd leaf design on the screen curtains. Magnus projectors and Brenkert arc lamps were installed together with British acoustic "Q:H." type Duosonic sound system, to reproduce a complete range of balanced sound "from a soft natural whisper to the roar of an earthquake's terror". It was claimed that electrical apparatus was duplicated so that in the event of breakdown the performance would not be interrupted. Ear-phones were fitted to 66 of the seats to "bring back the beauty of sound to those with bad hearing".

Banks of fresh water atomisers washed the incoming air to "exterminate Mr. Germ" such that the air breathed would be "as pure and wholesome as the keen sparkling air of the Swiss Alps". Some 100,000 gallons of water were needed daily to wash 23,000,000 cubic ft of air weighing 800 tons. The staff including page boys, wore uniforms in blue trimmed in lighter blue and silver.

The gala opening was formally performed on 30th May 1938 by the Mayor of Birkenhead, Alderman C. McVey, with the film star, Miss Nova Pilbeam as guest of honour. In order to fullfil her obligations to attend, Miss Pilbeam had defied her doctor who had considered she had not fully recovered from the effects of concussion which she had suffered in a taxi cab accident the previous month. Traffic jams were caused by the huge crowds that had gathered to greet the guest, some had waited six hours to watch both the arrival and departure of the celebrities. Other dignitaries present included the Mayor of Bebington, Alderman R. Milne who has accompanied by the Mayoress. The Mayor had more than a formal interest in the occasion for it was he who, in his business capacity of solicitor, had submitted the original plans for the cinema to the local magistrates for approval. The inauguration commenced with a fanfare by four scarlet-coated buglers from the 4/5th Battalion the Cheshires Regiment. After expressing thanks to all concerned with the project, particularly the workmen who had completed the task in just forty four weeks, the Mayor declared his appreciation of the fact that the town now had another modern cinema and he "hoped that in addition to preventing Birkenhead people from seeking cinema entertainment in Liverpool, the Gaumont would induce Liverpool cinemagoers to come to Birkenhead". The opening film was George Formby's *I See Ice*.

Programmes included daily matinees at 2.30 and evening performances at 6.15, whilst on Saturdays there were two distinct performances at 6.15 and 8.40. Prices ranged from 6d in the Front Stalls, 1/- in the Back Stalls, 1s 3d in the Back Circle and 1s 6d in the Front Circle. Children were admitted for 4d and 6d.

The Gaumont closed unceremoniously on the 4th January 1964 and the last films were Jane Lockhart, Hugh Reilly and Jon Provost in *Lassie's Great Adventure* plus Pat Boone, James Mason, Arlene Dahl and Diane Baker in Jules Verne's *Journey to the Centre of the Earth*. It was re-opened by Tommy Trinder as a Bingo and Social Club on Thursday April 16th that year with seats for 1,600. The building had been modernised with buffet facilities and electronic controls for the game. More recently the premises were converted into a Snooker Club.

BIRKENHEAD GAUMONT

PROGRAMMES

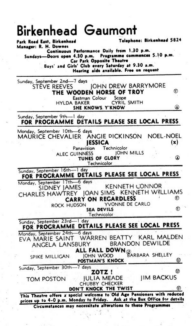

Birkenhead Gaumont

Park Road East, Birkenhead   Telephone: Birkenhead 5824
Manager: R. H. Downes
Continuous Performance Daily from 1.30 p.m.
Sundays—Doors open 4.30 p.m. Programme commences 5.10 p.m.
Car Park Opposite Theatre
Boys' and Girls' Club every Saturday at 9.30 a.m.
Hearing aids available. Free on request

Sunday, September 2nd—7 days
STEVE REEVES   JOHN DREW BARRYMORE
THE WOODEN HORSE OF TROY
Eastman Colour   Scope
HYLDA BAKER   CYRIL SMITH
SHE KNOWS Y'KNOW

Sunday, September 9th—1 day
FOR PROGRAMME DETAILS PLEASE SEE LOCAL PRESS

Monday, September 10th—6 days
MAURICE CHEVALIER   ANGIE DICKINSON   NOEL-NOEL
JESSICA (x)
Panavision   Technicolor
ALEC GUINNESS   JOHN MILLS
TUNES OF GLORY
Technicolor

Sunday, September 16th—1 day
FOR PROGRAMME DETAILS PLEASE SEE LOCAL PRESS

Monday, September 17th—6 days
SIDNEY JAMES   KENNETH CONNOR
CHARLES HAWTREY   JOAN SIMS   KENNETH WILLIAMS
CARRY ON REGARDLESS
ROCK HUDSON   YVONNE DE CARLO
SEA DEVILS
Technicolor

Sunday, September 23rd—1 day
FOR PROGRAMME DETAILS PLEASE SEE LOCAL PRESS

Monday, September 24th—6 days
EVA MARIE SAINT   WARREN BEATTY   KARL MALDEN
ANGELA LANSBURY   BRANDON DEWILDE
ALL FALL DOWN
SPIKE MILLIGAN   JOHN WOOD   BARBARA SHELLEY
POSTMAN'S KNOCK

Sunday, September 30th—7 days
ZOTZ!
TOM POSTON   JULIA MEADE   JIM BACKUS
CHUBBY CHECKER
DON'T KNOCK THE TWIST

This Theatre offers a special welcome to Old Age Pensioners with reduced prices up to 4-0 p.m. Monday to Friday. Ask at the Box Office for details
Circumstances may necessitate alterations to these Programmes

PINEWOOD STUDIOS CALLING

Everyone at Pinewood is very excited about the recently-completed picture "The Wild And The Willing" which is due to be released later this year. Starring Virginia Maskell and Paul Rogers, the film also introduces several outstanding young newcomers. A great screen future is already prophesied for Ian McShane who plays a tempstuous university student in "The Wild And The Willing" and Samantha Eggar is another who is expected to follow-up with other fine performances.

Others in the cast of "The Wild And The Willing" include Catherine Woodville, Johnny Sekka, who appeared in an earlier Pinewood picture "Flame In The Streets", and John Standing, recently seen in the comedy "A Pair Of Briefs".

"The Wild And The Willing" presents a slice of student life at one of Britain's provincial universities. The youthful cast combine brilliantly to show the hopes, dreams, ambitions and frustrations of the students. It is produced by Betty Box and directed by Ralph Thomas — the team who made such pictures as "No Love For Johnny" and the "Doctor" series.

Norman Wisdom, now making his ninth comedy for the Rank Organisation at Pinewood, has been creating not a little havoc in and around the studios. In one scene involving a hosepipe he managed to drench most of the film unit—and several bystanders too.

And while on location in nearby Windsor producer Hugh Stewart had a difficult job to keep Norman in front of the cameras. So many local residents asked the popular comedy star in for a cup cup of tea that filming was almost brought to a halt.

Published by Kine-Ads Limited, 74 Great Bridgewater Street, Manchester, 1
Printed by Clifton Printing Co. Ltd. Comford Road. Marton. Blackpool

Hippodrome

(Ohmy's Circus/Gaiety Music Hall/The Metropole)

Mr. W. W. KELLY, J.P., C.C.

The first theatre manager in Britain to open his premises to the wounded of the 1914-18 war.

In 1888 Ohmy's Grand Circus opened in Grange Road, Birkenhead. The origin of the name was attributed to the spectacular rope trick performed by the circus proprietor and famous balloonist, which culminated in him falling a considerable height causing the audience to gasp, "Oh My". The plans were for it to be run as a circus for part of the year and as a theatre for the remainder of the time. On these lines, however, the venture proved unsuccessful and within two years it was taken over by Mr. Ellis Brammell who converted it into a legitimate theatre when its name had changed to the Gaiety Music Hall. Then in 1898 Mr. W.W. Kelly became the lessee and the name again changed, this time to The Metropole Theatre. The theatre was then run with touring companies and melodrama. In 1908 the theatre was acquired for the De Frece Circuit syndicate with Mr. Walter De Frece's as director and Mr. Henry Ball the resident manager. The theatre closed for several months for alterations and re-opened on Monday 7th December of that year and its name had been changed yet again, this time to the Hippodrome Theatre of Varieties. The manager was Mr. Frank Weston (who later went on to open the Coliseum in Wallasey).

The premises had been renovated inside and outside. The mood inside was one of warmth and spaciousness. It had been designed so that every member of the audience had an unimpeded view, no matter what class of seat. Throughout the theatre fixed doors had been installed to obviate draughts, with no fewer than eleven exits to permit management to clear the building within three minutes in the event of an emergency. Tip up seats were provided in every part of the hall with the exception of the gallery. A total of 2,000 could be accommodated with comfort with seating capacity for 1,600. Velvet and plush was extensively used in the upholstery to provide an air of refinement. The stage had been considerably enlarged and equipped with the most modern accessories in the way of lighting, scenery, etc., and the Hippodrome was by now lighted throughout by electricity. In short, the management had spared no expense in creating one of the most luxurious theatres in the North of England. Finishing touches included the smartly turned-out attendants — "men in livery and women neatly gowned, aproned and capped". A high class fifteen piece orchestra provided the main musical items on the programmes. The theatre opened at 6.30 each evening for two houses, the first started at 6.50 and terminated at 8.40. Prices of admission were 3d in the gallery (for which there was no early door); Pit 4d (early door 2d extra); Balcony 6d (early door 9d); Circle 9d (early door 1/-); single seats in private boxes 2/-, and private boxes at 10s 6d and 7s 6d.

Hippodrome (circa 1912)

Large crowds gathered for the opening performance which had Miss Vesta Tilley (De Freces wife) top of the bill. The congregation outside congested the entrance and exits making access difficult and the long queues, which had developed some considerable time prior to the theatre opening, stretched to a point opposite the Baptist church. Even the roadway was choked with people and the police had some difficulty in keeping a narrow channel clear for carriages. Inside, the hall was decorated with flowers courtesy of florists Messrs. Mason and Co., of Oxton Road. Early in the evening Mr. De Frece went before the curtain and addressed the audience and begged their indulgence for any hitches that might have been noticed. These, he said, were due to the inexperience of some of the staff. All were Birkenhead men, he admitted amid applause, and some had not quite settled down to their new work. He declared that it was management policy to provide clean and wholesome entertainment to which men could safely bring their wife and daughters and he invited the public to assist by drawing attention to anything they considered objectionable.

During De Frece's reign the Hippodrome continued to be run as a theatre. Responding to the growing popularity of the cinema some theatres had been converted into picture houses (e.g. the Queens which had previously operated as a Music Hall for fifty years). In January 1914 the prospectus of a new cinema combine "Associated Provincial Picture Houses Ltd" included plans to acquire several properties for conversion into picturedromes, including the Hippodrome in Birkenhead. This appeared to come to nothing and by 1916 the theatre had been taken over by Dennis J. Clarke who had been responsible for much of the success of the Argyle Music Hall. The Hippodrome continued to be used primarily for live entertainment although there is some indication that a film of Jack Jolish training for a fight was shown in the early days. Between 1929 and 1932 cine entertainment was periodically included in the bill of fare at the Hippodrome. One of the first of these was *Simba*, a travel film depicting the adventures of Mr. and Mrs. Martin Johnson in Africa, with excellent shots of animals and half naked natives. It was unusual in having a synchronised talkie foreword by Mr. Johnson who explained how the film was made. It also received wide press coverage with full page spreads in the local papers and opportunities were provided for the "Chums" to attend free.

Eventually, however, in response to market forces the Hippodrome was converted into a "first class picture theatre" and the film selected for the re-opening on 31st October 1932 was Edgar Alan Poe's masterpiece *Murders In The Rue Morgue*.

The alterations to the exterior of the building had included 1,000 ft of neon lighting and a raised 'Hippodrome' sign 12 ft in height. Inside, a massive screen 500 sq ft in area had been erected and it was claimed that only one loom in the country was capable of weaving the screen in one piece and spraying it electrically to render it transparent. Rear projection equipment was used and the latest Electrical Western systems were installed. The inclusion of a microphone

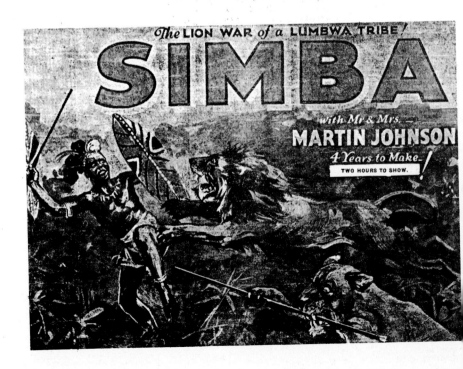

and loud speaker system to enable management to make announcements from their office to the audience was a novel feature claimed to be used in no other cinema in the country. A rectifier and stand-by generator were provided for the talking apparatus. By special arrangements patrons of the Hippodrome were allowed to use Robb Bros' car park free of charge and an attendant was on duty. According to 1935 data the seating capacity was 1,375.

The new manager of the Hippodrome was Mr. Frank Burbury from Nottingham and an orchestra provided musical entertainment under the direction of Mr. Abbot. The aim was to provide a mixed programme of talking films plus live stage shows which ran continuously through from 2.30 to 10.30pm. Within a couple of years however the Hippodrome was sold to the Birkenhead Co-operative Society for conversion into the town's largest store. The final programme on 10th March 1934 was 'Evening Follies' on stage. This proved to be a moving occasion and despite many curtain calls Alderman Clarke refused to address the audience who sang 'Auld Lang Syne' and the National Anthem, before leaving the premises to reminisce outside.

BIRKENHEAD

HIPPODROME

RE-OPENS

MONDAY, OCTOBER 31st.

D. J. CLARKE presents
LONDON'S LATEST CRAZE
A GIGANTIC

NON-STOP SHOW

CONTINUOUS 2.30 to 10.30.

ON THE SCREEN:

MURDERS IN THE RUE MORGUE

AN HOUR OF THRILLS.

ON THE STAGE:

VARIETY

LUPESSU SISTERS,
THE 2 ARTHURS. BILLY BARR
TOM FAGAN, RIGOLETTO TRIO.
WENSLEY and DALE.
SPLENDID ORCHESTRA.
SOUND BY WESTERN ELECTRIC.

NOTE PRICES OF ADMISSION.
(Including tax).

	BEFORE 5 p.m.		AFTER 5 p.m.	
Circle	1/3	Circle	2/-	
Stalls	1/-	Stalls	1/6	
Pit	8d.	Pit	9d.	
Family Circle	6d.	Family Circle	6d.	

Lyceum (1939)

Lyceum

Planning permission was granted in March 1913 for the erection of a picture palace at the corner of Grove Street and Olinda Road, New Ferry. The project was realised some months later with the grand opening of the Lyceum Cinema on 30th August 1913. Attendance at the opening performance at 3pm, was by invitation only. The programme comprised a special selection of musical items by the Lyceum Bijou Orchestra under the direction of Mr. A. Davies together with a wide range of films including *The Lighthouse Prisoners*.

The inaugural ceremony was conducted by Councillor J. McLeavy, of the Lower Bebington Urban District Council whose vision was that the Lyceum would provide entertainment, recreation, education and relaxation for local people after the heavy turmoil in the factories or the confinement of offices. Admission charges were from 3d to 1/-.

Lyceum (1939)

Lyceum (1939)

Staff at the Lyceum party

Birkenhead tramcar outside the Lyceum at the New Ferry terminus

The 1,176 seater cinema was designed by Messrs. Nagington and Shennan of Liverpool and constructed by Messrs. Waring and Sons of Derby. The chosen site was particularly convenient being as it was at the New Ferry tram terminus on New Chester Road. The directors were concerned over the technical quality of their films and had installed unique Imperial Model de Luxe projectors by Messrs. Pathe Freres. They were also concerned about the nature of the subject matter of the films and declared their intention to ensure that, under the capable hands of Mr. A.O. Thomas, nothing would be shown on the screen that would bring blushes to the most sensitive cheeks. In line with most write-ups on new cinemas it was claimed that everyone had a good view of the screen and the attractive picture house was well ventilated.

Towards the end of 1929 this south-end cinema was extended and artistically renovated on a lavish scale. Upon re-opening in mid December 1929 the film screened was *The Lion and the Mouse* with May McAvoy and Lionel Barrymore. The last silent film at the Lyceum was *Chinese Bungalow* with Mathieson Lang. Western Electric Talking machines were installed in March 1930 for the talkie premier on 10th March of *King of the Khyber Rifles* starring Victor McLaglen and Edmund Lowe. The sound reproduction proved to be superbly clear and distinct and the performance attracted record attendances.

In the late 1930's the Lyceum became part of the S.M. Super Cinema circuit and in 1939 it was completely renovated and decorated. The scheme included new light fittings throughout, a new stage proscenium and satin curtains with a special appliqué design. A minor gas explosion occurred in the house during a Saturday performance in 1949 but the packed cinema was safely evacuated within two minutes. In 1957 the management refuted rumours that the Lyceum was to close and pointed out that since the cinema had been taken over by the Essoldo group, it was company policy to change the name to New Ferry Essoldo. Indeed the new name had already been put on the front of the building. The Regal in Bebington had also been renamed Essoldo. The new owners, however, failed to prevent the Essoldo from closing a few years later mainly as a result of falling attendances and vandalism. Hundreds of seats in the stalls had had to be removed from the rows because of serious damage. The last film shown in March 1962 was *In the Dog House* with Leslie Philips, plus a Canadian second feature. Soon after, the building was converted into a supermarket, the plans of which had been passed before the cinema had closed.

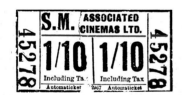

Lyric

(Walsh's Picturedrome/Price Street New Electric Picturedrome)

This Birkenhead cinema, which opened on Wednesday 24th April 1912 to a considerable crowd, was located between Watson Street and Park Street with its frontage on Price Street and its back on Queensbury Street. The Proprietor was Mr. Walsh and the premises became known locally as Walsh's Picturedrome. The hall, which had a seating capacity of around 500, was lofty and contained no galleries thus making it ideally suited for the purpose of showing films. Great attention was devoted to accident prevention: the operating room was built on the outside of the building, and there were exit doors both at the front and the rear of the hall. Performances were at 6.40 and 9.00 p.m. with admission at 2d, 4d and 6d, and at 1d and 2d for the children's matinee at 2.30 p.m. on Saturday afternoons. Programmes were changed twice weekly.

Although the opening programme is unknown, films on show by the second week of operation were *The Cowboy Bride* (a wild west adventure), *The Saving of the Special* (a drama depicting life on a Canadian railway and the bravery of the engine driver as he tried to save the 'special') plus a host of comedies which included *Max and his Dog, Dick, How to Avoid a Noise* and *Holding His Own*. It was the proprietor's declared intention to provide clean and pleasant entertainment for the neighbouring residents.

On the 30th December 1920 the Lyric Cinema (Birkenhead) Ltd., was set up with the aim of purchasing the freehold land and property known as Walsh's Picturedrome, together with the adjoining two shops. Incorporation of the latter into the upgraded premises enabled the seating capacity to be expanded from 550 to 900 and facilitated the provision of additional features including a waiting room. The refurbishments also included a new stone front, a new balcony and new entrances and exits.

The official opening of the re-christened picture house, planned for the 3rd October 1921, was delayed by one week. The attractive advertised opening programme included *With All His Heart* showing beautiful and picturesque views of the castled-home of the Bassingtons in England with scenes periodically shifting to Australia. Musical accompaniment was provided by a trio.

Apparently the cinema earned the reputation for attracting drunks from nearby public houses, and became known as the 'Stagger-In'. Talkies arrived at the Lyric on 25th May 1930 with Jack Oakie in the comedy *Hard to Get*. It closed as a cinema unannounced with the last advertised programme in November 1946 comprising Ellery Queen's *Penthouse Mystery* starring Ralph Bellamy and Anna May Wong and *Eve Knew Her Apples* with Ann Miller. After it closed the premises were used as an engineering works. Now the area has been developed beyond recognition with the building of houses and flats; the district being referred to as Queensbury Gardens.

Lyric (1920's)

Palace (Rock Ferry)

In 1877 a hall was built adjacent to the Trinity Wesleyan Chapel in New Chester Road, Rock Ferry by the Rock Ferry Skating Rink Co. Ltd., and the original enterprise was managed by Mr. William Manfree. By 1885 the skating craze had petered out and the premises were taken over first by the local brigade of the Salvation Army and then by St. Peter's Church, as a Mission Hall and Sunday School. In July 1911 the hall was sold by the Church Authorities for £2,000 to a syndicate with plans to convert the premises into a picture house. St. Peter's themselves, were to build a place across the road. The conversion from church hall to picture house was completed later in the year and the premises opened as the Electric Picture Palace on the 4th November with Mr. Fred Alderton as the first projectionist and Mr. James Mole as the first manager soon to be replaced by Mr. Edward F. Evans. The first regular pianist to provide mood music for the silent films was Mr. Percy de Haas.

The entire building had been remodelled and it was claimed to be one of the best fitted electric theatres in the district. The front of the hall was handsomely and solidly constructed from Portland cement decorated with fibre plaster ornamentation and the whole painted with white enamel. At night the exterior was illuminated by numerous electric lamps.

Many features had been installed which were uncommon in early conversions of church halls to picture houses. The seats were of the tip-up pattern upholstered in red plush. The floor was elevated such as to ensure everyone had an uninterrupted view of the screen. The seating capacity of 600 included 100 of the best seats in the balcony. The floor was covered in Axminster carpets and cork linoleum and the whole was artistically decorated in delicate colour shades. The operators' box was of fire-proof design and entirely separated from the audience, even the apertures through which the films were projected were fitted with automatic iron shutters. The hall was equipped with five emergency exits, all without steps, which enabled the building to be evacuated within half a minute. The building was heated by a hot-water system and ventilation was provided by electric fans.

The opening ceremony was conducted in the presence of the Mayor of Birkenhead, Mr. A.W. Willmer, and a large assembly of invited guests. On his arrival, the Mayor was met on the steps of the picture-house by Mr. Sley, the managing director of the company owning the picture hall, and was presented

Staff outside the Electric Palace Cinema, Rock Ferry, George Parker, the projectionist, is 3rd from left in the back row (circa 1914).

with a suitably-inscribed golden key which his Worship used to open the main door and duly announce the building open. He declared his hope that the cinema would be used both for entertainment and education and he was conscious of the need for people to use their leisure time wisely. At the end of the inauguration speech the vicar of St. Peter's proposed a vote of thanks to the Mayor.

The opening programme at 3.00 p.m. consisted of a wide range of animated pictures, and afternoon tea was served throughout the event. The premises were opened to the general public at 7.00 p.m. and the first films were *Corporation and the Ranch Girl* plus *Chinese Revolution.* Under the management of Mr. R. Sugden, there were two exhibitions daily at 7.00 and 9.00 p.m. with matinees on Monday, Thursday and Saturday when afternoon tea was served free to patrons in the dearer seats. Admission was at 3d, 6d or 1/- and programmes were changed twice weekly. In its early days, in an attempt to draw a regular clientele, admission to the balcony included a free cup of tea and a biscuit. Soon after opening, management of the Electric Palace were involved in organising a benefit matinee in aid of the widows and orphans of the Titanic disaster and soon the Palace became a favourite cosy cinema in the area. Saturday nights often saw queues of second house customers stretching down New Chester Road with the doorman outside keeping order.

In the early 1930's the Palace underwent extensive renovation and was converted for talking pictures. Later in the thirties the picture house became part of the North Western Cinemas circuit who carried out further renovations including installation of Holophane stage lighting to illuminate the silver satin festooned curtains. The Palace was one of the first cinemas in the region to obtain a licence to open on Sundays shortly after the Second World War. Mr Mitchelson, a regular visitor to the Palace, remembers the church community marching up and down outside the cinema waving placards condemning people attending cinemas on Sundays. It survived the ravages of the Second World War only to endure the slow process of post-war decline, when during the late 1940's a boldly-painted sign on the side of the building invited you to "Take Your Alice to the Palace". Unfortunately, too few Alices were treated to a visit and the cinema eventually closed unannounced with the last advertised films *The Naked Street* and *Great Sioux Uprising* appearing in the press in February 1956. Soon after the premises were used as a car sales room, first by Palace Motors (Wirral) Ltd., and later by Argyle Motors (Birkenhead) Ltd. The building still stands to this day, but in a less-splendid state than in its early cinema years.

Rio after renovation (1944)

Palladium

(Rio)

A company known as The Birkenhead 'Palladium' Picture Hall Ltd., was first registered to purchase the 'Reflex' picture house in Price Street in July 1913. The Palladium picture house, designed by the Liverpool architects, Messrs. Nagington and Shennan, was eventually built on the site of the former Conservative Club in Price Street, Birkenhead. This 800 seater picture palace was opened by Mr. J.T. Thompson on 29th November 1913. Because of its location it had a special appeal as a place of entertainment for those inhabitants of the north end of town, a large and growing population. However, being only a few minutes walk from Park Station it was also readily accessible to patrons from further afield.

Palladium (1920's)

The building was so attractively upholstered and equipped with the most up-to-date technology in terms of projection apparatus, ventilation and a hot-water heating system that it became one of the most comfortable picture halls of its time in Birkenhead. The balcony was somewhat of unusual design being extended down one side of the hall, presumably to facilitate access and/or to provide additional seating.

In opening the cinema, the Mayor marvelled at the tremendous strides in design of the recently-built picture halls. The prophesy that the picturehouse craze would soon end was shown to be false and the Palladium continued to provide entertainment as a cinema for over thirty five years, first in private hands and in its latter years as part of he S.M. Super Cinema circuit and then the Essoldo Circuit Control in 1954.

In its early days during the First World War, stirring patriotic songs were sung at the cinema and local church choir boys are reported to have sang (out of sight) whilst the actors mouthed the words in silent films: musical accompaniment was by piano, sometimes augmented by a violin. From newspaper advertisements the first talkie at the Palladium appears to have been Colleen Moore's *Smiling Eyes* on 16th June 1930, but this is unconfirmed.

The Palladium was one of the several picture houses in the town that suffered severe structural damage during the war-time blitz when bombs exploding in Duke Street and Price Street in 1941 blew away a side wall in the cinema and loosened the girders in the roof. Ironically the final film on the night of the disaster was entitled *Phantom Raiders*, a Nick Carter detective thriller about a crook sinking ships mysteriously and drawing the insurance money. He was eventually apprehended by Walter Pidgeon as Nick Carter.

The extent of the bomb damage and the subsequent vandalism by children playing in the ruins prevented any temporary repair. As a result substantial renovation was undertaken by a Liverpool firm before the war had ended. The new cinema opened as the Rio on the 3rd July, 1944.

Rio after renovation (1944)

The resulting effect was pleasing but compared to its predecessor, the Palladium, the quality of the finish at the Rio was inferior and, by necessity, one of war-time austerity. Thus, instead of lush carpeting, the floor was covered in cement and asphalt. This was justified as being not only more hygienic but indeed bullet proof! In place of the sumptuously-upholstered seats at the Palladium, the Rio auditorium was fitted out with polished wooden seats. However, not withstanding the difficulties encountered during the war in obtaining materials and the consequential utilitarian design, the building was considered attractive and even 'cosy' in its early days. The walls were of deep rose merging into cream and etched with green, while, the golden silk curtains seemed to add an air of luxury. The cinema had a seating capacity of 600 with a small circle of 74 fully-upholstered seats.

The opening passed without ceremony with Mr. Southan Morris and Mr. S.W. Banks the Managing Director and the area supervisor respectively of S.M. Cinemas, attending the matinee performance. The programme consisted of an American 'short', the news, and the colourful hit production *The Girls He Left Behind*, a wartime love story starring Alice Faye and the Brazilian bombshell, Carmen Miranda.

Picturedrome

Roxy

It was announced on the 23rd November 1910 that a company, the Birkenhead Picturedrome and Billiard Hall Ltd., had been formed with the objective of acquiring the land and the six dwelling houses numbered 38-48 Salisbury Street, and to erect on the site a combined Picturedrome and Billiard Hall with its frontage on Whetstone Lane, Charing Cross. This was a prime site because of its central position both in relation to the local population and by virtue of lying on one of the busiest tramcar routes in the town. The directors of the new company were Mr. George Proudman, Mr. Robert Rawland, Mr. Edwin Haigh, and Mr. Robinson Franklin Hindle. The architects were the Southport based firm of Messrs. Campbell and Fairhurst who were well experienced in building picturedromes. The cost of the construction and fitting out was estimated to be £2,400. The proposal was for a high-class establishment such that "ladies and their daughters could attend without misgivings". The promoters' plans also included provision for delivery of fresh flowers daily to the cinema by a Birkenhead nursery man. The building itself was designed such that the sports facility was below, and entirely separated from the picture house by a massive sound and fire-proof concrete floor supported on wrought compound girders. The Company recognised that picture houses had "come to stay" and had educational values, despite the feelings expressed by others that picturedromes were a passing fancy.

The six dwelling houses were demolished, the site cleared and the Picturedrome and Billiard Hall duly erected. The Picturedrome began in the days when the Theatre Royal, The Argyle Theatre, The Hippodrome, and Saronie's Electric Theatre at the entrance to Birkenhead Park were the town's principal places of entertainment. Both the cinema and billiard room were opened on Thursday 25th May 1911 with the inauguration ceremony for the former taking place at 2.30 pm in the presence of the Mayor and Mayoress, Councillor and Mrs. A.W. Willmer, and that of the billiard parlour as a separate event in the evening. The latter comprised the finals of a league match between employees from Messrs. Cook and Townsend of Liverpool and Messrs. Robb Bros of Birkenhead. The match was followed by refreshment and a dance. The hall was available to both men and women players and, at the time, it was claimed to be the first billiard parlour to be illuminated entirely by electricity.

At the inauguration (which took place whilst workmen were still on the premises) the proprietors, (with Councillor George Proudman — Mayor of Birkenhead from 1911-1912 as Chairman and Mr Edwin Haigh as Managing Director) described the picture house as "the best appointed picturedrome in the North of England, luxuriously furnished, replete with every comfort, lighted throughout by electricity and by far and away the finest pictures in the country". The management explained their intention to make the Hall a place for physical and intellectual entertainment.

Councillor A. W. Willmer

The building indeed was sumptuously finished with handsomely upholstered tip-up seats, ornate fittings, lush carpets, brilliant electrical illuminations, "motor driven ventilating fans" and "special heating apparatus". The sloping floor feature provided a perfect view of the screen for the 550 audience. The interior was described as "compact".

Twice-nightly performances (6.45 and 9.00 p.m.) were in vogue at the time with 3 o'clock matinees on Mondays, Thursdays and Fridays. Admission charges were 4d, 6d and 1/- with afternoon tea or ices served free of charge in the 6d and 1/- seats. Entrance to Saturday matinees was 2d for school children. After the First World War prices were slashed to 3d, 6d and 9d with seats as cheap as 1d for matinees. The first programme proper included:

* *The Gaumont Graphic*, described as "a moving newspaper with pictures of all the latest events".
* *Picture of Tunis*, the city of white.
* The annual elephant race at Perah.
* A range of films, both humourous (eg *Cat and Dog, Davy Jones in the South Seas*, and *Betty and Jane at the Theatre*) and dramatic (eg *A Sprained Ankle* and *Doctor Cupid*). The pictures were both clear and steady and the general quality was considered to be good.

As a result of rising overheads and a dwindling local population due to migration to newer properties in other parts of the town, the Rio in 1956, like many of its contempories, was up for sale. Although it continued in use as a picture-house for another twelve months it finally closed in April 1957 with a showing of Edward G. Robinson's *Illegal* and *It's Magic*. At that time there were fourteen former cinemas on the market in Wirral and those which had recently closed in Birkenhead alone included the Super, Astor, Roxy and Regent. The building remained unwanted for many years and it was not until 1962 that it was sold by private treaty by Worsley and Worsley of Hamilton Square and became the Roxy Bingo Hall which survived into the 1980's when it finally closed and was demolished in 1987.

Roxy Bingo Hall, Price Street

Artist impression of Picturedrome

Roxy up for sale (1957)

After a ten-day period of closure in 1930 for redecoration and installation of British Thompson-Houston sound equipment, on the 10th June the Picturedrome became Birkenhead's latest recruit to talkies. The first sound picture, *The Gold Diggers of Broadway* starring Winnie Lightner, Conway Tearle, Ann Pennington and Nancy Welford, attracted a full house for the opening week. The foyer had been redecorated and set out with light-brown grained marble dado (which harmonised well with the marble staircase), darker skirting boards and a frieze which faded gradually from delicate pink to cream. The ceiling was also in cream with designs in ochre. Inside the hall itself the decor was of a similar scheme: the walls were artistically finished with Grecian figures in white relieved on a blue background. The panellings were in dark brown. New ventilation equipment had been installed. The popular manager, Mr. A.E. Parry, was praised by the critics for the quality of the building and the sound reproduction.

The cinema was prosperous for some time but it became less fashionable with the arrival of the larger cinemas. In 1935 the cinema was again refurbished and renamed the Roxy after being taken over by Mr. Harry Buxton (the father of Angela Buxton a well known tennis player) who had earlier won a fortune of £6,000 at the tables in the South of France. The seating capacity was recorded in the 1930's as being 1,000, almost double that when the cinema first opened. The plan was for non-stop shows between 2.00 and 11.00 p.m. and in the longer term for it to become a television theatre to receive TV news from the Alexandra Palace transmitter. Alas, these ambitious plans were not to be and Mr. Buxton relinquished his interest and the cinema became part of the SM circuit and latterly the Essoldo chain. Sometime during the 1930's an operator was tragically killed in an accident in the projection room.

In March 1956 the cinema was saved by the cleaner, Mrs. D. Edge, from serious damage. She was cleaning the circle when she noticed smoke and fire in the stalls and promptly called the fire brigade which fortunately was only a few doors away. The manager, Mr. P. Park, attributed the cause to a cigarette left smouldering from the previous night. Three seats and floor boarding were destroyed. Later that year the cinema was to close and a few years later became a store for the Birkenhead and District Co-operative Society, and more recently a sports shop. The former billiards hall had long ceased to be used for its original purpose and had been leased for fire brigade civil defence training who continued to use it for a short while after the cinema had ceased business. This was one of the first cinemas to close in Birkenhead during the rapid decline of the industry in the 1950-60's.

Picture House

(Super)

The old Super premises as they stand in 1989

In the early 1900's the intention was to construct a public hall on the site of the former old Post Office in Conway Street, Birkenhead. However, these plans fell through and when an application was made to the licensing authorities for permission to erect a picture house in a more central position in the town, there was considerable opposition. The main arguments were that there existed already a plethora of cinemas and that at time of war it was inappropriate to proceed with ventures which had the prime objective of amusement. Notwithstanding the objections, the licensing bench were eventually swayed and concluded that perhaps one more cinema could be accommodated in the town centre.

The splendid 'Picture House', as it was modestly designated, opened at the Argyle end of Conway Street in Birkenhead on the 26th June 1916. The front elevation was designed in neo-Greek style by the architect Mr. T.T. Rees. Taking cognisance of war-time economy the frontage was adapted almost wholly from material obtained from the old Post Office. Electrically driven ventilation fans and cleaning equipment were a feature. It had a seating capacity of 730 and on one occasion the entire audience was safely evacuated in under two minutes when a fire started in the projection room during a full house; fortunately the fire was contained.

In all, this was considered yet another luxury cinema for Birkenhead and was soon dubbed a 'Super' cinema. The inauguration ceremony was carried out by the Mayor, Mr. James Merritt who hoped management would ensure that the standard of programmes would be conducive to the good morals of young people.

Proceeds from the opening performance were donated to the Mayor's charities and the programme consisted of an adaptation of Arthur Pinero's *The Second Mrs. Tanquery* with Sir George Alexandra as Aubrey and Miss Hilda Moore as the highly emotional Paula. This feature was accompanied by the comedy *Fatty Tumbles into Toil* plus a number of war films including the memorial service for the heroes of the Jutland Battle. Excellent music was provided throughout by the Bijou orchestra led by Mr. Alfred Delmonte.

Following the introduction of talkies to Birkenhead, first at the Scala then soon after at the Empire, the Super initially resisted the trend and indeed claimed the superiority of the silent movies. By the end of 1929, however, the newspaper advertisements for the Super stated that talkies were on the way, a theme which continued weekly until 17th March 1930 when the first talkie screened was *Blackmail*. This gripping story of love and intrigue was supported by a film of the Oxford boat crew. A few months later the manager, Mr. Beaufort, moved to the New Brighton Tivoli and on the 21st June 1930 the Super licence transferred to Mr. H. Finnis. Around this period the cinema became part of the Gaumont British circuit. In response to the disastrous cinema fire in Scotland on the 1st January 1930, which took the lives of seventy children (see Coliseum), an emergency evacuation of some 700 people was rehearsed at the Super the same month.

Cinemascope was installed in the mid 1950's but the Super eventually closed in 1956 with the last advertised programme of Donald O'Connor in *Anything Goes* plus *Innocents in Paris* appearing at the end of September. The premises were converted into a ball room at considerable expense but soon that too closed and the building is now a furniture store.

Plaza

As early as 1913 interest was expressed in erecting a hall at the corner of Kingsland Road and Borough Road for cinematographic shows, music and dancing. The plans were to accommodate 900 with 200 seats in the balcony and 700 on the ground floor. However the application met with fierce opposition on several counts. Concern was expressed about the deleterious effects of the pictures on eyesight. Evidence was presented to the contrary by a doctor who also suggested that watching films could be soothing for the nerves. Head teachers were worried about the bad influence of the cinema on children and others thought that the traffic hazards posed by the double sets of tram lines on Borough Road made the site unsuitable. The outcome was that the magistrates refused the application and residents had to wait almost two decades for a cinema to be built in the area. In fact it was not until the end of 1928 before the Birkenhead Licensing Justices granted a license to Mr. Andrew Boyd to build a cinema on Borough Road between Carlton Road and Kingsland Road. The estimated cost of construction was £50,000, half of which was allocated for local labour. After some initial difficulty in getting 27 caravans moved from the site Messrs. Bennett Bros. of Hoylake began construction of the picture house but at a final cost nearer £100,000. By July 1930 the licence was transferred from Mr. Boyd to Mr. W.J. McAree.

The long-awaited luxury Plaza cinema eventually opened on 2nd August 1930, the ceremony being conducted by Alderman T. McLellan, Mayor of Birkenhead, with the Mayoress in attendance. Such was the importance of the occasion that the Mayor had interrupted his holidays in Scotland to attend the inauguration, and he was suitably impressed, remarking that the Plaza was undoubtedly the finest cinema in Birkenhead and probably one of the best in the North of England. It was considered to represent a milestone in the history of the development of British cinemas and with a seating capacity of 2,500 it was the largest picture-house in existence on Merseyside.

Plaza (1930)

Plaza vestibule (1930)

Plaza foyer (1930)

Whilst the external classical-style architecture, by A. Ernest Shennan, was not particularly striking, the cinema was undoubtedly a magnificent place of entertainment. The 180 ft frontage was constructed in red sand-faced Sibeley brick and finished in artificial cream cast stone to highlight the main decorative features such as the cornices, capitals, etc. The side and rear were faced with pressed Ravenshead bricks. The main central entrance was flanked on either side by illuminated panels and covered overhead by an illuminated canopy. Inside the theme was one of opulence based on wood finish, marble and concealed lighting: indeed not a single light bulb was exposed.

The main entrance through walnut doors led into the walnut-panelled vestibule which housed the pay-box and booking office plus a public telephone. Behind the vestibule was a wonderful 122 ft long by 20 ft high foyer lined with tavertine marble. The colour scheme was of ricn amber with coverings of modern-day tapestry with shades of green and petunia, and the entire foyer was subtly lit by concealed lights. The walls above marble dado were finished in a novel plastic paint and the radiator and window grilles were painted to mimic verdigris bronze. Perhaps one of the most striking features of the foyer, which has left a lasting imprint on the memories of those who use to frequent the cinema, was the ornamental wall fountain and niche, also in marble and mosaic with bronze head gushing water. At either side of the foyer, communicating doors led to a wide crush hall which gave easy access to all parts of the stalls, and a marble staircase led up to a tea lounge and 700 seater balcony.

Again the auditorium was of modern design and the general atmosphere was one of spaciousness and height, achieved by elimination of all overhanging ornaments and the designing of a second higher-vaulted ceiling. Walls were finished in a rough plaster above a dado of Bottoceni and black Cotticine marble

57

to a height of ten feet. The ceiling itself was covered in silver leaf and blue. The carpet and seat covers were sumptuous and the whole atmosphere was one of elegance. The 1,680 seats in the stalls were fixed in rows of separate level tiers. Beneath the balcony at the rear of the stalls the lighting was of golden sunshine enhancing the blue of the 'sky' above. The general lighting of the auditorium was mainly by means of cornice reflectors and French light fittings which could be controlled both from the projection room and from the stage. Much attention was given to detail as exemplified by the provision of sockets for fitting the ultra modern vacuum cleaners used for cleaning the cinema and which was considered to be somewhat of an innovation. Plenty of emergency exits were provided which led through an ante-room to the street.

The 40 foot wide, fluted proscenium opening was flanked by ornamental lights and the drapes of mercerized mohair were in three colours. A double-sided asbestos, fire-proof curtain closed off the stage. The Plaza boasted a magnascope screen capable of showing small pictures yet able to be adapted for a thirty seven foot picture. In addition to being designed for both the talkies and the silent films, the stage was equipped for traditional forms of live entertainment. A rising and falling platform was installed which was large enough to carry a twenty-two piece orchestra and the conductor plus a giant Compton organ, and was arranged such that the three lifts could operate independently. The organ was the largest on Merseyside and consumed 50,000 cubic feet of air per hour. In order to create the highest quality sound the organ pipes were enclosed in two large, sound-proof rooms, and to reach the theatre the sound had to pass through wooded louvres which were controlled from the organ key board; when closed, they became a solid wall. The cinema was designed with acoustics in mind.

Plaza (1930)

Mr. Frank Gordon at the Plaza organ

Plaza (1930)

Plaza cafe (1930)

On the first floor a large tea lounge and rest room with soda fountain provided an added attraction, tastefully decorated in stem-green and daffodil-yellow, with crystal-glass shades suspended from the ceiling by long silver supports. Adjoining the rest room was a walnut-panelled 'crush-hall' where second house patrons could wait, and, as mentioned earlier, a similar hall was provided on the lower floor. These facilities, together with the provision of the outside canopy, plus cloakrooms (where coats and hats could be left — an unusual feature of local cinemas), two public telephones, and toilets on each floor reflected the attention given to customer's comfort in the design of the building. Spacious offices were available for the manager and manageress.

The heart of the building, the projection room, and associated smoke loft, rewinding room and the 'non-sync' room (beneath the projection box) were fitted with iron fire-resistant doors. Two talkie and three silent film projectors were installed using Western Electric sound apparatus. The electricity supply was from the town's main and an innovation was the provision of an emergency lighting supply powered by electric batteries rather than gas. As with most modern cinemas of the times the heating and ventilation systems were considered to be the best with incoming air being washed in a plenum room in the basement such that the air in the auditorium was claimed to be cleaner than the outside air. The heating and ventilation equipment was installed by Sulzer Bros. of London and the painting was undertaken by Charles A. Cain of Sparks Lane, Thingwall. Beck Windibank carpeted and seated the premises.

The management team included Mr. William John McAree (appointed manager on behalf of Bedford Cinemas, 1928 Ltd.) with Mr. J.F. Wood as Managing Director (previous controller of the Queens Hall Cinema in Birkenhead from 1905 to 1928). The opening programme consisted of organ recitals and a host of films (including *The Last of Mrs. Cheyney*, a famous successful talkie, *A Perfect Day* with Laurel and Hardy, *Patch Pictures* a silent cinemagazine, *Hello Baby* a coloured talkie, *When the Cat's Away* a Mickey Mouse cartoon, plus *Plaza News*. The orchestral performance under the director of music, Mr. Louis Cohen, consisted of Sir Edward Elgar's rousing march 'Pomp and Circumstance', Wagner's 'Rienzi' and Strauss' haunting waltz 'The Blue Danube'. In addition to providing a sound of its own the Compton impressively mimicked a wide range of musical instruments such as the xylophone and triangle, and realistic effects of a song bird, steamboat whistle, roar of the surf, drone of aircraft, etc., thus making it a versatile accompaniment to the silent pictures. Soon after the opening, Hugo Rignold took over as Director of the Plaza Symphony Orchestra. Mr. Oddy was organist and he became a popular figure at the Plaza. After his death Sydney Gustard took over and in 1938 he in turn was replaced by Frank Gordon from Paramount, Manchester who stayed until 1951 prior to moving to the Ritz. Mr. Gordon remembers with affection his times at the Plaza and such film epics as Nelson Eddy/Jeanette Macdonald versions of *The Vagabond King, Naughty Marietta* and *May Time* together with many Fred Astaire/Ginger Rogers classics.

During the War the Plaza cinema was bombed but after a short break for repairs it reopened in April 1941.

From the mid 1960's the Plaza held bingo sessions on and off for about seven years but changed full time to bingo in January 1969. However, on the opening night there were only 400 players and the following month the Plaza reverted to a cinema with bingo sessions on Thursdays and Saturdays only. The demand for bingo had been misjudged, the reason being attributed to the plethora of bingo halls that were already available in the town. Its later success as a picture-house however was limited.

Like many cinemas in the town during the latter half of the century, the Plaza experienced rising costs at a time of declining attendances. In 1971 after a recent £10,000 modernisation programme, theft and vandalism by children outstripped profits from matinees. As a consequence, management charged unaccompanied children adult prices. Towards the end of its life as a picture house, the Plaza played second run Rank and ABC releases. During its final years as a cinema "Projectomatic" equipment was installed which automatically linked the film to the operation of the stage curtains, auditorium lighting, and the start-up of the incoming projector.

By early 1973 an application was made to convert the Plaza from a cinema into a full bingo hall. Despite petitions the owners, Bedford Cinemas, stated that whilst daily attendances of 1,000 were essential to make the forty three year old 2,500 seater cinema viable, these takings had been realised only once in the first seven weeks of 1973 and average daily attendances were actually below 150. Inevitably the North West's largest cinema closed as a picture house on the 3rd March 1973 and the final film was *The Good, the Bad and the Ugly*. Within two days workmen moved in to commence the £100,000 conversion. The premises reopened as a Mecca Bingo club which survives to this day. The small electronic Compton organ used at the bingo sessions is a far cry from the giant Compton in the days of Louis Cohen and Frank Gordon.

Queen's

The Queen's Hall Theatre at 19/21 Claughton Road, Birkenhead (at the corner of Kendal Street) opened on the 21st January 1862. (The Conway Arms public house was built in 1873 directly opposite the theatre but this was demolished in 1968 to make way for the tunnel approach flyovers). In 1908 a series of exhibitions of animated pictures were presented at the Queen's. The first was on the 29th January by the Northern Cinematographic Trading Co., from the Palace, New Brighton and then again on the 9th March by the Columbria Animated Picture Co. The latter programme was described as "Bright and Sparkling" and included a film of the wrestling match for the 'Catch as catch can' world championship between George Hackenschmidt (The Russian Lion) versus Joe Rogers of America. Also screened was *The Band Contest*, the latest and most humerous production by Pathe Freres of Paris, with realistic stage effects and introducing many of the popular songs of the day. The cinematographic items were supplemented by live variety which featured Harry Plant (comedian and musician) and Gilroy (a renowned ventriloquist). Admission was at 3d in the Gallery, 6d in the body of the hall, second seats at 1/- and front seats at 1s 6d.

The Queen's Hall closed around 1912 and after extensive alteration work re-opened as the Queen's cinema on the 10th November 1913. The picture-house was a tall building with its Claughton Road frontage covered by a cast iron roof above the pavement to protect queueing patrons in inclement weather.

Queens Hall to the right of the Ritz (Essoldo) (1963)

The interior was hardly recognisable after the transformation. The old Queens had its 'ground floor' upstairs with a series of smaller rooms below which had been used for meetings of friendly societies. So that a respectable seating capacity of around 1,300 could be provided, some lateral thinking went into the plans for the reconstruction. Thus the small individual ground floor rooms were demolished to make way for a vast auditorium. In order to make the building more lofty than would have been possible by merely reconstructing what was originally above the ground, extensive excavations were necessary with recourse to an amphitheatre style of construction with the ground floor constructed on an inclined plane ensuring the 500 seats had an unobstructed view of the screen even from the rear of the hall. The balcony was designed on the same principles as the auditorium. Further economies of space were achieved by building the projection room quite apart from the main building. This also had the advantage of insulating the theatre from the otherwise unavoidable noise of the projection equipment. Seats were of the tip-up arm chair variety sumptuously upholstered in velvet and the floor was lavishly carpeted.

The provision of extra exits made sure that everyone could be evacuated in a couple of minutes. The profusion of electric lights attracted attention in the early cinema as did the use of electric fans to "purify the air".

On behalf of the proprietor, Mr. J.F. Wood, the manager, Mr. H.M. Brennir claimed that the quality and character of the pictures shown at the Queen's would be the best. The first week's programme included the Western, *The Battle of Elderbush Gulch* plus *Mysterious Eyes, An Unwritten Chapter*, and *Broncho Billy and the Western Girls*.

Whilst the Ritz (Essoldo) next door developed the reputation of being the grandest cinema in town, the Queen's was one of the best loved. Admission was at $2^1/_2$d downstairs and 5d in the balcony. Programmes, which started each evening at 8.00 p.m., with 3.00 p.m. matinees on Thursdays and Saturdays, were changed each Monday and Thursday. Such was the arrangement of cinemas in that part of town that if you missed a film at the Gaumont or Super you catch it at the Queen's. One early recollection of the Queen's was of the bombardment of the audience in the stalls by cigarettes, match boxes, orange peel etc., from the balcony. The Queen's on the other hand, did also have the reputation for high quality pictures at reasonable prices.

By the time of the First World War the cinema was considered to be an old building and from then on its appearance became progressively jaded as a result of age and neglect. General Theatre Corporation (GB) had taken over the ownership of the Queen's by 1930 when talkies were installed, the first advertised talkie being Marie Dressler and Rudy Vallee in the musical *A Vagabond Lover*. By this time performances began daily at 3.00 p.m. with the evening house between 6.30 and 10.40 p.m. Admission charges had changed little over the years with entrance now costing 3d to 6d for the matinees and 4d to 1/- in the evening. Indeed the price of the dearest seats did not increase up until the Second World War.

The final closure of the Queen's as a cinema around the middle of 1949 was a quiet affair with the last advertised programme, *Portrait From Life* with Mai Zetterling appearing in the 25th May edition of the local paper. In 1952 plans to convert the building into a dance hall were approved by the Birkenhead Planning Committee but by the 1960's the premises lay derelict and were eventually demolished for the land to be used as a car park.

Regal

The £50,000 1,316 seater Regal Cinema on Bebington Road near Dacre Hill, was uniquely situated in a part of the peninsula where cinemas were scarce. The plans originally showed the seating capacity for the balcony to be 510 but the licensing magistrates insisted upon the provision of three additional gangways. This effectively reduced the number of seats to 479. At the same time, however, an extra row of seats was installed on the ground floor to increase the capacity from 766 to 837. The cinema opened its doors on the 12th February 1938 as the latest member of the SM Super Cinema chain in Birkenhead. Like the Ritz, which opened four months previously, it was a particularly fine example of the modern architecture of that time. The architect, Mr. Sidney Colwyn Foulkes, had been responsible for several cinemas in North Wales which included the 'Regal' at Rhyl. The first manager was Mr. Val Tress who had 20 years previous experience in the industry.

Set back from the road, its frontage was displayed to best advantage with a forecourt laid out in lawns and planted with shrubs. Imposing archways, leading to a spacious rear car park, flanked the building on either side.

The premises were constructed from grey brick with ferro-concrete reconstructed stone dressing on ground that sloped sharply downwards such that the access to the balcony was basically from the same level as the foyer. This tended one to underestimate the height of the building. A spacious canopy extended across the entire front of the cinema to provide shelter for customers queuing outside. At night the front of the building was floodlit in red.

Regal (1938)

Regal (1938)

Regal (1938)

Regal (1938)

Two entrances led from the 60ft x 32ft foyer to the balcony circle with the minimum of steps whilst the auditorium was approached via a lower foyer by an easy descent from the main foyer. The two foyers could accommodate the entire audience in the event of inclement weather. The main spacious foyer was almost the full width of the building and the foyer ceiling was covered with numerous tiny concave silvered circles to reflect multicoloured lights hidden in a series of troughs along the side walls and above the entrances to the circle at either end of the foyer. Originally, the architect intended that this lighting be controlled by an auto-cyclo Holophane unit, similar to that used to control the auditorium lighting, but this idea was rejected on the grounds of expense.

The interior design was essentially one of simplicity, and the style of the auditorium was claimed to resemble that of a Greek amphitheatre, with the walls forming a semi-circle in the centre of which was the stage flanked on either side by six large silvered columns. The outward curvature of the stage contrasted with the concave nature of the architrave. The exit doors beside the stage were concealed in alcoves between the columns such that they were invisible from the auditorium proper. The design was conceived with the aid of the Holophane Company Ltd., to give full scope to the sophisticated Holophane moulded-contour lighting system, the function of which was to enable the auditorium to be flooded in a constantly-changing array of colour from sources of illumination hidden aloft in the ceiling, concealed in front of the balcony and in side alcoves and in the wings of the stage. Signs of the zodiac were picked out in silver on the architrave above the stage. Besides exploiting the visual effects the design of the cinema interior was also dictated by the acoustical requirements and the comfort of its patrons. The upholstery was in grey with matching luxurious carpeting. The heating, ventilation and air conditioning systems were also given high priority.

The main stage curtains were executed in silver velour with two appliquéd bands of pale blue satin just above the fringe along the lower edge of the curtain, whilst the screen curtains were in festooned silver satin. Stage lighting consisted of footlights, overhead batten and vertical battens at either side of the stage. The opening film was *Topper* with Ronald Young, Billie Burke, Cary Grant and Constance Bennett.

On October 5th 1938 Mr. Southan Morris, the controller of the leading chain of independent cinemas in the country, which owned the Regal, announced that, because of the popularity of the Regal and requests from customers, a Compton Theatrone cinema organ was to be installed in the Regal. The organist, Harry Croudson, was an accomplished musician and a regular broadcaster on radio. At the time he was resident organist at the Ritz and was previously with Paramount Theatre in Manchester and, before that, with the Majestic in Leeds. His simultaneous appointment at the Ritz meant that between performances he had to dash by taxi from one cinema to the other.

In later years four of the columns flanking the stage were removed to accommodate a new wide screen and the installation of fluorescent lighting in the foyer seemed to detract from the glamour of the original arrangement.

In January 1957 it was announced that the Regal would change its name to Essoldo in line with company policy. Both the attendance figures and the condition of the premises declined in subsequent years; in the winter of 1969 the heating system failed completely and closure came a few weeks later on the 22nd February with a showing of Peter Cushing in *Corruption* plus *Dead or Alive*. After standing derelict for a short time the building was demolished and the site cleared for the erection of a supermarket.

Regent

Regent cinema (1948)

Regent waiting room (1931)

Regent (1931)

The Regent cinema in Birkenhead was situated between a block of shops and a public house on Church Road, Higher Tranmere. The proprietors were Tranmere Picture House Ltd., with Mr. J.J. McDonnell as manager at the time of opening on Monday 16th July 1923.

The main waiting room in the central hall was large and tastefully finished with artistic decorations and mahogany panels. A less imposing waiting room was used for access to the cheaper seats. Such was the arrangement that all exits from the main hall led direct to the street so that customers leaving the building were not impeded by second-house patrons in the main waiting room queuing for entrance.

The principal colour scheme of the main hall was white with crimson plush upholstery, thick green carpets and rich velvet screen draperies and curtains embellished in gold. Hanging from the white decorated ceiling were eight large lights fitted with handsome rose du Barry shades. This was supplemented either side by tiny flame-coloured lights. The raised floor ensured a good view of the screen from any of the 1,100 seats; there was no balcony.

The fire-proof operating room was designed to the best standards and the modern projection equipment avoided picture distortion and eye strain. The heating and ventilation system ensured that the air was cool during hot weather (such as the heat wave experienced at the time the cinema was opened) and warm in the winter.

Regent (1931)

Regent cinema being demolished (1972)

A musical introduction by the Regent Symphony Orchestra under the direction of Clyde Lewis was followed by the inauguration speech by the Mayor, Councillor J.W. Collins who was accompanied by his wife. The Mayor congratulated the management on bringing the cinema to a part of the area which was quite some distance from the town centre. Noting that the opening performance was free to invited guests the Mayor 'suggested' that management should at the earliest opportune time organise a benefit show in aid of hospitals and other charities. The idea was warmly approved by the audience. Following a second orchestral selection, the principal films shown were 'Forget-me-not' and 'The Bashful Sailor' plus a film of the erection of the Regent itself and showing its management and staff with subtitles based on *The House That Jack Built.*

Evening performances were continuous from 6.30 to 10.30 p.m. and matinees were provided on Monday, Thursdays and Saturdays. Admission charges were claimed to be very moderate at 6d, 9d and 1s 3d and the 9d and 1s 3d seats could be booked in advance at no extra charge. The musical sessions on Tuesdays and Fridays were set aside for requests from the audience made the previous week. An innovation was the periodic flashing of the time on the screen to help make sure that patrons did not miss their buses.

Compromise, a comedy college story starring Eddie Quillan, a relative new-comer to the silver screen, was the talkie premiere at the Regent on the 10th March 1930. The acoustics of the house proved to be well suited to talking pictures and the Western Electric installation provided faithful sound reproduction. Just prior to the change over to sound, the manager, Mr. John Winnal took up a post in St. Helens and the Regent licence was transferred to Mr. Douglas A. Hinds. The early thirties also saw the Regent become part of the Associated British Cinemas Group. After an uneventful life the Regent closed its doors for the last time in December 1956 with a showing of *My Teenage Daughter*. This was the fifth Birkenhead picture house to close since the war and the property was offered for sale with assessed rates of £730. As with the Astor, the Town Planning Committee decided that they had no interest in purchasing the property and eventually the building was demolished to make way for a garage and Auto Safety Centre.

Rialto

The inauguration of the Rialto picture-house was formally performed on the afternoon of 27th July 1933 by the Chairman of Bebington Urban District Council, Mr. J. Marshall. Mr. J. Wilson, Clerk and Solicitor to the Council was also in attendance. The house was packed when it opened to the public the same evening. The first programme comprised *Rialto News, Tea for Two* (a Warner Brothers Technicolour Review) and the spectacular musical *Tell Me Tonight*.

This cinema was conveniently situated facing Port Sunlight village at the corner of Bebington Road and Alma Street, near Bebington station. It served a thickly populated urban area which was to expand still further over subsequent years. The need for a cinema in the area had been recognised for some time. Despite the first-rate bus services Bebington was a considerable distance from the centre of Birkenhead.

The modern and imposing facade was constructed in plum-coloured rustic brick and white glazed faience with a wide, decorative canopy covering the white, glazed main entrance. The 'house' interior was even more luxuriously finished than the outside. The main vestibule and steps were covered by white Sicilian marble. Access to the auditorium was via a spacious waiting room covered in Hopton wood terrazzo. The main staircase, which led to the balcony foyer and balcony proper, was similarly finished in Hopton wood terrazzo and rich carpets. In the auditorium the simplicity of the decorative plaster work enhanced by subtle use of lighting was a striking feature. The colour scheme was of amber, rose and silver. The proscenium draperies were also of rose and silver effectively illuminated by a system of four-circuit colour footlights blending together automatically to produce a futuristic yet fairyland quality.

Rialto (1933)

The balcony construction was somewhat novel in that it did not project over the rear stalls. This removed the claustrophobic and depressing atmosphere often experienced sitting under a low ceiling, as well as assisting materially in the ventilation of the building as a whole.

Luxurious and comfortable fauteuils in rose-coloured velvet with sponge rubber arm rests provided roomy seating accommodation for 1,275 visitors. Mr. Albert E. Askew, a well-known Merseyside musician of the time, provided the music on the latest patented all-British Compton organ. This instrument sported a glass console which was illuminated from within in a riot of constantly-changing colours. The console itself was positioned centrally in front of the stage and no lift platform was provided.

The sound equipment was a Western Electric model and the operating room, which had a separate exit to the street, contained the latest in projection hardware and a hand-winch to operate the stage curtain.

A low-pressure hot-water system heated the building. Foul air was extracted by powerful electrically-driven ventilation fans, whilst fresh air was introduced into the house through grilles located at various heights. A car park with capacity for about an hundred vehicles was sited at the rear of the cinema which was accessed via Alma Street.

The Rialto finally closed mid-1961 with a showing of Michael Craig and Billie Whitelaw in *Payroll* plus *Clue of the New Pin*. The building was then utilised as a removals and storage warehouse before being more recently converted into Breaks snooker club.

Rialto (1933)

Rialto (1933)

Ritz

Monday 4th October 1937 was a red-letter day for the townspeople of Birkenhead, for this was the day when Britain's foremost star of stage, screen and radio, Gracie Fields, came to open the "Showplace of the North", as the new Ritz cinema had already been christened and which was heralded as the finest theatre outside the West End of London. An estimated 75,000 fans lined her route to the cinema around Conway Street, Claughton Road and Argyle Street, causing traffic jams and requiring extra detachments of police to divert traffic. On arrival Gracie signed autographs (including the shirt of the Ritz's manager which was then on display for several weeks in the window of the local press offices) and she delighted fans before the ceremony when she emerged through a window above the main cinema entrance to sing the opening lines from 'Sally' and conduct the crowds as they joined in.

The Ritz was situated on an island site at the corner of Claughton Road and Oliver Street, on an area of over an acre. The main frontage was faced with white Portland stone, the grouped windows and doors forming a contrast to the plain surfaces of masonry. On the corner over the main entrance, a circular steel and glass tower rose to about seventy feet above the ground and was well illuminated from the inside at night. (During the war the tower carried an air-raid siren.)

Robert Cromie, F.R.I.B.A., the architect, had been responsible for the design of many leading theatres in Britain, Europe and America. Notable examples include the Davis Theatre (Croydon), the Gaumont Palace (Hammersmith) and the Prince of Wales (London). He had planned the Ritz foyer to give access as direct as possible to all parts of the theatre without having recourse to corridors. The main entrance was through a group of glazed doors at the corner of the building surmounted by a blue and gold canopy measuring 67ft x 3ft 6in. The

Ritz (1937)

Ritz paybox and cloakroom (1937)

pay-boxes were accommodated on either side of the doors in the vestibule, through which one entered the large foyer which was decorated in shades of peach and gold with mirrored pillars and topped by a magnificent coffered ceiling picked out in blue with lighting domes edged with gold. Facing the entrance doors was the grand staircase branching off to the right and to the left on the first landing to a large balcony foyer. The wall at the head of the staircase was completely covered by mirrored glass. From the balcony foyer there was access to the front of the balcony and to the centre cross-gangway of the balcony. Also on the first floor there was a large cafe which had concealed lighting in the shaped coves of the ceiling. The cafe was operated by Reeces and was used by business men from Hamilton Square as well as by cinema patrons.

Cinema accommodation was provided for nearly 2,500 in the auditorium. The latter was 130 ft. long and 95 ft. wide with a throw from projection room to screen of about 150 ft. Auditorium decorations were in a warm shade of peach blending with the terracotta shades of the carpets and the deep rose of the seating. One of the features of the decorations was that the lower parts of the walls up to dado level were covered in plain, dark plum-coloured carpeting. Above dado height there was modernistic mural relief provided by heavy-textured plastic paint in shades of gold, red and brown with detailed features picked out in bright blue; tubular light fittings added to the decorative effect on these upper side walls. All the main lighting was concealed and towards the front of the theatre was a series of five lighting coves which continued from ceiling down the side walls, the rays from the lamps being projected towards the stage. Another lighting cove served to illuminate the proscenium surround with three-circuit colour lighting, the only ornamentation to the surround being provided by the close grille work at the side of the stage with corresponding ventilation grilles above the proscenium, which was 56 ft. wide and a little more than half as high.

Ritz (1937)

Ritz (1937)

The stage itself was 75ft wide and was fully equipped for the presentation of the most elaborate stage shows, even though the local planning committee had stipulated that the height above the stage should not exceed that of the auditorium roof, thanks to the intervention of Councillor Clarke who owned the nearby Argyle Theatre. He feared that the Ritz might be used for full-time stage shows in opposition to his own famous variety theatre. This then made it impossible for the screen and scenery to be used in the usual fashion. Cunningly, however the base of the screen was fitted with small rollers which enabled it to be moved back stage along grooved tracks in the stage floor. The quilted satin main curtains were in five colours in gradually lightening shades, whilst other draperies were executed in gold, flesh-colour and bottle green. Included among these was a silver satin contour curtain that could be draped into a variety of shapes for use during stage presentations and organ interludes. Stage lighting was provided by Holophane Ltd. who supplied a float and three battens. Side floods were also available and the projection room equipment included two Stelmar spots. A three-piece safety curtain was supplied by Merryweather & Sons Ltd. adorned with a painted festoon curtain design. John Compton & Co. supplied the £10,000 four-manual organ with illuminated console and 'Electrone', the console being on a lift in the centre of the orchestra pit. The organ pipes varied in length from a few inches to 16 feet and the chambers were beneath the stage. Projection was by two Super Simplex projectors with Peerless Magnarcs and Western Electric Mirrophonic sound. A bi-unial lantern was also installed in the projection room.

Great play was made of the uniforms worn by the Ritz staff. They had been designed in London and were unique in the theatre world. The blue velvet outfit of the fourteen girl attendants was cut in the style of the French hunting season with hobble skirts partnered by tight fitting jackets edged in gold fleur-de-lys design fastened with gold buttons to match those trimming the gauntlet cuffs. The costume was finished with frilly white lace cravats and Cromwellian shoes with red and gold buckles and red heels. In addition, the management also provided silk stockings and a free hair style. The outfits of the three door attendants and little page boy were of a deep blue doeskin and of gold fleur-de-lys pattern. The two receptionists wore a uniform made from the same material comprising short jackets and revers of satin.

Ritz 'showpiece of the north'

The opening programme, attended by the Mayors of Birkenhead, Liverpool, Bebington and Wallasey and Viscount Leverhulme, commenced with the Gaumont British News, followed by the ceremony conducted by Gracie Fields · with the Bach Trumpeters of H.M. Royal Military School of Music, The Ritz Orchestra and the 14 Ritzettes. After this, Reginald Foort introduced and demonstrated the Compton Grand Organ, playing *Rhapsody in Blue, Indian Love Call, Trees and Zampa,* the first letters of which spelled out the cinema's name. This was followed by a Popeye cartoon called *The Painless Window Washer,* then the stage presentation with Jan Ralfini and his Broadcasting Band, the famous Dagenham Girl Pipers and Drummers, Steffani and his 21 Singing Songsters, Falls Reading and Boyce, Eddie Windsor (Compere) and the resident organist Rowland Tims. Finally came the feature film, *The Man in Possession* starring Robert Taylor and Jean Harlow. Also present at the opening was W. Southan Morris, managing director of S.M. Super Cinemas Ltd. & Associated Companies, to whose rapidly expanding circuit the Ritz had now been added. Gaumont British News filmed the event and a few days later audiences at the Ritz could see Gracie Fields on the canopy outside the theatre serenading over a thousand onlookers. (This film remained in the projection room at the Ritz for many years: does anyone know where it is now?)

For several weeks in May 1937, during the building of the Ritz, the Directors of Cheshire Picture Halls took the opportunity to solicit the views of cinemagoers regarding any aspect of film entertainment by publishing a questionnaire in the local paper. So great was the response from readers that the prize was increased from one to four guineas. They even received a reply from a lady on holiday in Sussex. The results, which provided a completely-new insight into patrons tastes, helped to influence the planning of entertainment at the new cinema.

In the three years that followed, manager Bill Boht spared no efforts to justify the title "Showplace of the North" for his theatre. He was a true showman for whom nothing short of perfection was acceptable. It was due to his enterprise that arrangements were made with the Empire Theatre in Liverpool that scenery, draperies and lighting equipment could be borrowed; the Paramount in Liverpool, whose cine-variety policy had been virtually abandoned by the late thirties, also were prevailed upon to loan equipment. Stage shows with all the best known dance bands and variety artistes were presented at regular intervals, with organ interludes at other times featuring famous broadcasting organists. Often, more trouble was taken in the presentation of these interludes than most other cinemas or theatres would take with a full stage show!

In September 1938 a new resident organist, Henry Croudson, came to the Ritz from the Paramount Manchester and two weeks later he simultaneously became resident organist at S.M.'s beautiful new Regal Cinema in Bebington Road, Birkenhead, where a Compton Theatrone electronic organ had just been installed. Immediately after his interlude at the Ritz, Croudson would be rushed by taxi to the Regal, less than ten minutes' drive from the Ritz on the outskirts of Birkenhead, where he was always a very popular addition to the film programme. From October 17th Croudson was even busier, this time conducting his own seven piece orchestra on stage at the Ritz together with attractive blonde singer Lesley Walsh. For these shows the organ console was removed from its lift and placed on the stage in order that Croudson could become part of the band. Even Sunday was no day of rest for Henry Croudson, for he was again conducting his orchestra on stage at the Wallasey Gaumont Palace, where Sunday concerts were a feature of the winter season. They also appeared on stage at the Regal in November of that year. Of course, famous broadcasting bands were regular fare at the Ritz, and Bill Boht believed that Jack Jackson's Band had by far the best stage show of any band that appeared at

★ **CinemaScopE** ★

A BREATHTAKING
NEW WORLD OF
SIGHT,
SOUND & COLOUR
WITH
THE WONDROUS
MULTIPLE TRACK
" MAGNETIC
STEREOPHONIC
SOUND !
PRESENTED BY THE

FEBRUARY

Programmes at Birkenhead Cinemas owned by S.M. (August 1939)

the Ritz. He described him as a "real showman" — praise indeed from Mr. Boht — and said he thought it very unfair that Jackson received far less for his appearance than the more famous Henry Hall, of whose showmanship Mr. Boht obviously did not approve.

1939 saw regular broadcasts from the Ritz from Henry Croudson, and in May of that year he staged his first 'Chums on Parade' show at the Regal with local juvenile talent. He also found time to write a weekly children's column in a local newspaper masquerading as 'Uncle Henry'. A further 'Chums on Parade' was due to appear in addition to the film programme at the Regal at the beginning of September and 'Uncle Henry' informed his readers that additional stage lighting equipment and props were being supplied by the managements of the Ritz and Paramount to make this an even better show than last time, but unfortunately an even more important 'show' was due to commence in Europe on the third day of September — the Second World War.

The outbreak of war caused all cinemas and theatres to be closed for two weeks till September, 18th, which was to be Croudson's last week at the Ritz before departure for military service. Alex Taylor was the next resident organist at the Ritz, though he didn't have to play the Regal organ which was moved to the Winter Gardens, New Brighton, at the end of the year with Alan Lusty as organist. Henry Wingfield followed Alex Taylor at the Ritz in November 1939 and stage shows continued at regular intervals. In June 1940 Robinson Cleaver took over.

A visit to the Ritz in the summer of 1940 is recalled as follows:

It wasn't just the thick carpet that almost enveloped you as you stepped into the foyer, or the magnificently uniformed doormen and page boys, nor even the usherettes in their 'French Riding Habit' uniforms that impressed patrons, it was the whole atmosphere that made you immediately aware that this was not just another cinema — but was THE cinema! Everything seemed more opulent and different, even in an era when almost every cinema set out to impress its patrons with a 'super cinema' image. Preceding the screening of the big picture, several sets of curtains parted to reveal the words 'Ritz Presents' before the main title appeared and most memorable was the moment when the organ console rose into view and the tabs opened to reveal a magnificent stage setting. This gave the impression of a 'heavenly dream' sequence from a Hollywood musical, with various shapes resembling clouds being flooded with slowly changing colour lighting. When Robinson Cleaver reached the finale of his interlude, the usual sing-a-long with popular hits of the moment, a song sheet with the appropriate words appeared from above the stage and into the audience came two little page boys with microphones, and patrons were invited to sing-a-long with Mr. Cleaver. Even at this weekday summer matinee there was a packed house, and no wonder with a show such as this!

Another vivid recollection of a visit to the Ritz was recalled in an article that appeared in the local press some years ago. It was December 21st 1940, when a youthful telephonist named Evelyn Atkins and her boyfriend Jimmy Brown went to the Ritz for their Saturday night at the pictures. The film was *Stardust* with Linda Darnell and John Payne, plus Florence Rice and Kent Taylor in *Girl in Room 313*. At the organ was the current resident organist, Harold (B.B.C.) Hunt. Evelyn remembers that it was a busy night and they were looking forward to an enjoyable evening and a pleasant Christmas — a Christmas helped along by the £10 bonus Jimmy had handed to Evelyn for safe keeping and which now lay in the pocket of her fox fur coat.

At about seven, the audience stirred and grumbled as a message was super imposed on the screen: "An air raid is now in progress and those who wish to leave are asked to do so calmly". Few people did leave and the show continued without further interruption until the normal finishing time of 9.00 p.m., this early finish being a feature of those days when air raids were an almost nightly occurrence. At the close of the film, manager Bill Boht came on stage to advise the audience that the air raid was still in progress and those who wished to were welcome to remain in the theatre until the 'all clear' sounded. After this the organ console again rose into view and Harold Hunt commenced his by now all-too-familar duty of entertaining patrons above the noise of the Ack Ack barrage and exploding bombs. Some people did leave the theatre, but many remained, and Evelyn and her boyfriend were among those who moved seats, choosing two near the back, beneath the dress circle for greater protection. As time went by, a few patrons left the theatre and returned with fish and chips from a nearby shop, but Evelyn and Jimmy remained in their seats, though by this time she had become stiff in the joints from leaning one way for too long and asked Jimmy to swop seats — a move that was to save her life. Only minutes later a bomb crashed through the roof of the auditorium just forward of the circle and exploded with devastating effect plunging the theatre into complete darkness. The sound of the organ had been replaced by screams from the audience, and Sally Eglington, the chief usherette who was descending the stairs from the cafe carrying a cup of tea to Harold Hunt's dressing room, was killed by flying wreckage. Further below, beneath the dress circle, which had buckled in the middle and where ten people lay dying, Jimmy Brown was clutching the back of his head and Evelyn was reassuring him: "We're all right, Jim. We're all right."

He clutched his head tightly as she half-pushed, half-carried him over rubble and bodies through the black, scream-filled auditorium, out into the open and along the road to the first aid post in Conway Street Elementary School thirty or so steps away. There, when the hands were removed from his head, the back of Jimmy Brown's head fell away, and Evelyn was told he must have died the instant the shrapnel or wreckage hit him as he sat beneath the breeched circle. She still wonders how a dead man could walk to a first aid post. There were nearly one hundred casualties at the Ritz on that night, and a second bomb outside the building had shattered the rear wall.

The architects M.W. and W.M. Shennan of Birkenhead were commissioned to prepare plans for the restoration of the theatre, and in 1944 a permit was granted for the repair of the rear wall and for the roof to be re-asphalted, but it was not until July 1946 that permission was granted for the work of reconstruction to be carried out in real earnest. Two of the main girders, each 90ft. long were badly twisted and, to replace these, 50ft. of roof had to be removed. Surprisingly, the grand foyer was virtually untouched and even the mirrors remained intact, but the auditorium needed extensive remodelling and replacement of fibrous plaster throughout. The original contractors, Messrs. Lloyd and Cross, declined the job, and problems were experienced in this austerity-ridden year of 1946 in obtaining materials and craftsmen to do the restoration.

In most respects the restored auditorium resembled the original, but the tubular light fittings were no longer a feature of the side walls adjacent to the circle, while a large shaped panel was placed on each side wall in 'tapestry' style with gold wallpaper on which a design had been painted. The fibrous plaster proscenium surround had lost its fluted effect and at either side were now grilles built up of a series of tubes finished in gold. Three-colour lighting was again provided for the surround by coloured lamps controlled by auto-cycle dimmers, but problems were experienced with inadequate light being cast onto the grilles, so the coloured lamps were replaced at either side by two vertical magazine battens taken from the side of the stage at the Regal, which had survived the war unscathed.

A second-hand three-manual Christie Organ, reconditioned by Wurlitzer, that had been originally installed at the La Scala in Glasgow was brought in to replace the badly damaged Compton, and an orchestra lift was added that would increase the stage depth by 15 ft. when raised. The presence of this seldom-used lift, was given as the reason for not installing footlights in the renovated theatre, but it was claimed that sixteen spotlights housed in the balcony front together with three at either side with remotely-controlled colour filters, would adequately replace the float. As usual with such claims, it was found in practice that the 'flat' lighting from these front-of-house sources did little to enhance the folds of stage draperies, which was always the main function of the footlights in the cinema. Other lighting was provided by overhead and side stage battens.

A new curtain was supplied by G.B. Kalee, made of heavy gold satin, appliqued with various coloured satins. Light satin curtains were fixed to the main screen trolley, which was electrically controlled and designed to travel upstage when the stage was required for shows. No cloth was available for other 'tabs', so a false proscenium was built in sections on the stage. This had a steel framework and was faced with silver and gold wallpaper on which a design was painted, the side and top sections being moved into required positions by electric motors. The original contour curtain, repaired and renovated, was back in use for the re-opening.

An unusual feature of the new installation was a subsidiary reefing screen at the front of the stage that could be dropped in order that a short film could be shown to bridge the gap while the stage was being prepared for live presentations. This screen was in six five-foot sections which enabled it to be

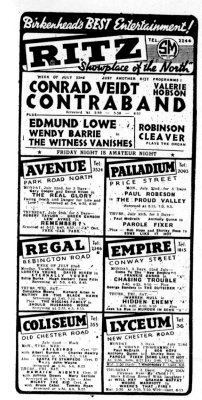

Programmes at the Birkenhead cinemas owned by S.M. (July 1940)

Showing programme at Ritz at time of bombing (December 1940)

81

Stage show at the Ritz (1938)

accommodated in the area above the stage when not in use. Extra speakers were provided behind the side grilles and above the proscenium for service on occasions when the front screen was in use. The new projection equipment consisted of two G.B. Kalee 21 projectors and Westrex sound equipment.

The re-opening scheduled for the 13th January 1947 created great interest. The second opening featured the Band of the 22nd (Cheshire) Regiment with trumpeters of H.M. Royal Horse Guards. Film actor Frank Lawton participated and Robinson Cleaver, assisted by Molly, was at the organ. An *In Town Tonight* feature was compered by Movietone News commentator Lionel Gamelin, himself a native of Birkenhead, and footballer Dixie Dean was one of those interviewed. The famous operatic star Gwen Catley was next on the bill, followed by Bill Cotton and his band, after which the film programme commenced with British Movietone News followed by the Merseyside premiere presentation of the latest Fred Astaire/Bing Crosby film, *Blue Skies*. This time the event was recorded on film by Movietone. Tickets were fixed at two and one guineas in the Circle and the whole of the stalls sold at 5s and 2/6. All of the box office takings were donated to charity: 75% to the Birkenhead General Hospital in recognition of their fine rescue efforts on the night of the air raid and the remaining 25% were given to the Cinematographic Benevolent Fund.

Bill Boht was soon back at the Ritz and the policy of regular stage shows and featured organists continued as previously well into the early 1950's. On the eve of the outbreak of the war government restrictions prevented the Ritz from using their display of neon lights. These restrictions were not lifted until 2nd April 1949 when, as dusk fell, the lights were switched on again for the first time in nigh on 10 years, with the exception of the re-opening night in 1947. A big occasion at the Ritz later in 1949 was a 'Replica Royal Command Performance' at 8.00 p.m. on Monday the 21st November, when Southan Morris was there to welcome a galaxy of well-known film stars including Bebe Daniels, Ben Lyon, Valerie Hobson, Christine Norden, Richard Todd, John McCallum, Margaret Lockwood and Gregory Peck, for the provincial premiere of *The Forsyte Saga*, starring Greer Garson, Walter Pidgeon and Errol Flynn. The equally star-studded stage show that preceded the film was compered by Ben Lyon and included Leslie Hutchinson (Hutch), Nat Allen and his orchestra, Wilson, Keppel and Betty, with Reginald Foort at the organ. Highlights of the event were recorded on film, by Pathé.

Henry Croudson and his orchestra with Lesley Walsh (1939)

After the war the Ritz suffered two fires, one in 1952 in the paint store near the balcony and one in 1956 in the boiler room. Fortunately neither caused any serious damage and the cinema was able to open as usual. To mark its 14th Anniversary a huge 200lb cake was baked in the form of a model of the cinema and distributed to early lady patrons at matinee performances throughout the special week.

For a time, Gordon Banner was resident organist but was obliged to depart rather hurriedly after being cited in a divorce case that received considerable publicity in the local press. An immediate replacement had to be found and Frank Gordon was persuaded to leave his post at the nearby Plaza and become the last resident organist at the Ritz. By 1954 steeply-falling audience figures had forced cinema owners to turn to the expensive gimmickry of wide screen, CinemaScope, etc., in an effort to woo the public away from their new television sets. However, Southan Morris was sufficiently astute to realise that the downward trend would continue unabated, and negotiated the sale of almost his entire circuit, reputed to be the largest independent group in the country, to Essoldo. It is said that he would have liked to have retained his 'flagship', the Ritz, but Essoldo insisted that this theatre be included in the deal.

Soon after the takeover Frank Gordon revealed that he had no illusions as to what his future prospects would be and was consequently seeking to transfer his activities to the management side, though eventually he decided to continue his musical career outside of the cinema industry. Bill Boht was also soon to leave the trade for which he had done so much, and the demise of the Ritz rapidly accelerated through what seemed to be an almost deliberate policy of neglect. When the end finally came, virtually no part of the mechanical equipment in the theatre, outside of the projectors, was still in operable condition, and 'tabs' were rarely used due to the anxiety that once closed they might fail to open again.

What was billed as a "Farewell (Temporary) Performance" came on Sunday the 5th January 1969 when, for that one night only, the double feature programme was *The Body Snatcher* with Boris Karloff and Bela Lugosi and *The Amazing Colossal Man*, after which the Ritz was to close for 're-decoration and modernisation'. Despite this announcement, however, the Ritz was not destined to re-open as a cinema.

During its heyday for around 1s 6d one could see top bands and personalities (e.g. Billy Ternant, Cyril Stapleton, Geraldo, The Beverly Sisters, Diana Dors) plus two feature films, and musical interludes plus special guest appearances by the stars. A three-course meal could be obtained at the restaurant for 1s 6d. Nowadays the Ritz operates as a Bingo Hall run first by Ladbrokes and then more recently by Top Rank who spent £500,000 in 1988 on refurbishments.

Wartime damage at the Ritz

Ritz cafe (1947)

Ritz foyer and grand staircase after refurbishment (1947)

Ritz after refurbishment (1947)

Ritz reopening ceremony (13th January 1947)

Savoy

Plans for this £40,000 — £45,000 cinema were passed by the magistrates in August 1936. It was estimated that it would take eight to nine months to construct and the project would involve demolition of the Scala together with a number of houses at the rear of the cinema. The seating capacity would be greatly enlarged and the frontage would take in the motor show-room and the shop that flanked the existing premises. It is somewhat surprising that when this new, large, upmarket cinema at 51/53 Argyle Street in Birkenhead did open on Monday the 10th October 1938, the occasion passed without ceremony surprising because of its size, its status, and its history.

The building stood on the site formerly occupied by the Theatre Royal and subsequently the well-liked Scala cinema. By any standard the Savoy was large in comparison with the town's existing picture palaces: it could hold an audience of around 2,100 (compared with 970 at the Scala) and the seating capacity of 768 in the circle alone exceeded the total seating accommodation of many picture houses in the area. The de-luxe cinema was tastefully finished with luxurious

Savoy cinema (1939)

fittings. The spacious stalls foyer was decorated in light beige relieved with delicate shades of green and thick red and gold pile carpet. Pendant lights in the lounges and main hall provided just the right amount of illumination whilst small footlights were set at intervals in the passages. The numerous little side windows were hung with velvet 'box' curtains to give a quaint cottage effect. Although there was no organ at the Savoy the well in front of the platform and lattice work on the walls either side of the stage indicate that plans had catered for this provision. Similarly, although the Savoy was built with the sole purpose of showing films, the size of the stage accommodation suggest contingency plans for live entertainment. The stage draperies consisted of maize-coloured satin tableaux curtains, trimmed in floral design coloured satins, plus festooned screened curtains in maize satin and matching 'legs' and 'borders'. High quality Ross Kinematographic projectors were installed to ensure pictures were clear and steady, and the RCA Sound equipment provided acoustics that enhanced the illusion of reality. Attention was given to the fire precautions with a fire-proofed projection room and, despite the size of the cinema, ample emergency exits were installed so as to enable the entire building to be evacuated within two minutes. A free car park was provided for the use of customers. The manager, Mr. J.C. Kennedy, with some twenty years experience in the business in Liverpool and London, opened the cinema with the Ernest Lubitsch success *Bluebeard's Eighth Wife* starring Claudette Colbert and Gary Cooper.

Savoy interior (1938)

Savoy cinema under EMI just prior to closing

In 1956 Mr. S.D. McAree (ex Regent cinema in Old Swan, Liverpool) became manager of the Savoy when Mr. M. Wright, manager since 1954 and twice in three years champion manager for the Liverpool District of Associated Cinemas, was promoted to manager of the Regal in Putney.

The Savoy became the ABC in 1961, and in line with many picture houses in Wirral bravely fought in vain against the inevitable decline in attendances with late night films etc. The circle had been abandoned for eleven years when the cinema finally closed its doors in March 1982, making its eighteen staff redundant. Although the staff held a farewell party the sadness of the occasion was reflected by the manager at the time, Mr. Ray Vautrino, who observed that not one of the 160 patrons leaving after the final performance made any passing reference to its closure.

In August 1982, the building was on offer at £100,000 and soon became the town's first modern snooker hall.

Everyone is Reading

ABC FILM REVIEW

containing

FULL COLOUR STAR PIN-UP
STAR INTERVIEWS · CROSSWORD
FASHION PAGES · CARTOONS Etc.
THE LATEST ISSUE NOW ON
SALE AT THIS THEATRE

ABC

SAVOY . BIRKENHEAD

Programme for

APRIL

SUN	MON	TUE	WED	THU	FRI	SAT
1	2	3	4	5	6	7
8	9	10	11	12	13	14
15	16	17	18	19	20	21
22	23	24	25	26	27	28
29	30					

SAVOY : BIRKENHEAD Telephone : Birkenhead 2738

Monday, February 4th ———————— for six days
Marlon Brando : Jean Simmons : Frank Sinatra : Vivian Blaine
GUYS AND DOLLS (A)
(CinemaScope : Eastman Colour)
Monday, February 11th ——————— for six days
Glenn Ford : Jeanne Crain : Broderick Crawford
THE FASTEST GUN ALIVE (A)
James Cagney : Barbara Stanwyck : Walter Pidgeon
THESE WILDER YEARS (A)
Monday, February 18th ——————— for six days
William Campbell : Marian Carr
CELL 2455, DEATH ROW (X)
Rhonda Fleming : Ricardo Montalban
THE SLAVE WOMAN (A)
(Technicolor)
[Persons under sixteen not admitted to any part of this programme]
Monday, February 25th ——————— for six days
Jimmy Edwards : Laurence Harvey : David Tomlinson
Shirley Eaton
THREE MEN IN A BOAT (U)
(CinemaScope : Eastman Colour)
Bruce Bennett : Richard Arlen : Faron Young
HIDDEN GUNS (U)

SUNDAYS AT THE SAVOY

———————— Sunday, February 3rd ————————
Robert Stack, Joan Taylo. ———— Warpaint (Pathe Color) (A)
Lew Ayres, Nancy Davis ———————— Donovan's Brain (A)
———————— Sunday, February 10th ————————
Jane Powell, Farley Granger ... Small Town Girl (Tech.) (U)
Rod Cameron, Tab Hunter ———— Treasure Of Kalifa (U)
———————— Sunday, February 17th ————————
Billy Daniels ———————— Cruisin' Down The River (Tech.) (U)
Greer Garson, Walter Pidgeon Scandal At Scourie (Tech.) (U)
———————— Sunday, February 24th ————————
James Cagney, Doris Day, Virginia Mayo ... Fine And Dandy (U)
Martha Hyer, John Bentley ———— Scarlet Spear (Tech.) (U)

CIRCUMSTANCES MAY MAKE CHANGE OF PROGRAMMES NECESSARY

Theatre Royal
(Scala)

On the 31st of October 1864, in the presence of the town's MP Mr. John Laird, the Theatre Royal opened at 51/53 Argyle Street, Birkenhead, four years prior to the opening of the Argyle Theatre in the same street. The architect was Mr. Lewis Hornblower of Birkenhead and the design was such as to provide accommodation for 2,300 although only 1,850 were seated. The opening address was written by Mr. William Brough but presented by Mr. Alexander Henderson under whose management admission charges were 1/- in the gallery, 1/6 in the pit 3/- in the boxes and 4/- in the dress circle. On the 24th June 1892, fire caused £2,000 worth of damage and the closure of the theatre for a while. Upon re-opening it had been re-decorated and fitted out with new upholstery, but it was closed again in 1905 for more extensive alterations which included the installation of electric lighting. The modernisations were completed in time to enable the theatre to re-open for the August Bank Holiday that year. During the refurbishment an old spring well which had been covered up was discovered below the stage, thought to be one of Birkenhead's early water supplies.

Cinematinees were introduced into the programmes at the Theatre Royal in May 1910 and early pictures taken by Messrs. Weisker Bros. of Liverpool covered the funeral of King Edward VII. In order to shed some of his business pressure, Mr. W.W. Kelly, last leasee of the Theatre Royal, sold the premises to Messrs. Sol and Alfred Levy, owners of some sixteen to eighteen cinemas in the country. The location of the building in a part of the town where the population density was high and where there were few places of entertainment made this an attractive site for a cinema.

Theatre Royal – an early view

Thus by the 1920's the popularity of live theatre had given way to the movies and in order to respond to this shift in taste of entertainment, the Theatre Royal closed on the 8th January 1921 with the last performance of the play *Romance*. The guests for the evening included the Mayor, Councillor Luke Lees and the Mayoress, Miss Dorothy Lees. This was a sad occasion for some as it represented the end of an era. Mr. and Mrs. Kelly, who had owned the Theatre for a quarter of a century said farewell on the stage after the final curtain: Mrs. Kelly had often entertained wounded soldiers home from the war.

The new proprietors spent a fortune in converting the theatre in to a modern picture house. Indeed the installation of the electric organ itself cost around 3,000 guineas. Imaginative effects were created by artistic use of lights and the whole atmosphere was one of luxurious spaciousness. One major problem encountered during the refurbishment was in providing adequate office accommodation but in the end this was also successfully resolved.

On entering the new theatre from the street there was a well-proportioned hall of classic design, on the right-hand-side of which was the main stairway to the balcony, cafe etc. On the newel post (or central pillar) was an ornamental ruby red brazier balanced by two similar lights on opposite walls. Entrance to the stalls was via a screen of pillars and the main lounge hall. The latter was of Neo Graeco influence and sported artistically-illuminated semi-archaic panels of black murals depicting Greek legends. Indeed the foyer had a temple-like atmosphere.

On passing into the auditorium the most noticeable feature was the proscenium. The projection equipment was somewhat novel to the area with the films being projected from behind the stage rather than from in front of the screen. This necessitated the screen being transparent to the film yet opaque in terms of the audience not being able to see either the projectionist or his equipment.

The brightly decorated stage was set off by glowing blue background. The proscenium opening was flanked by two tall piers, colossal guilded masks and decorative, lacquered lanterns. Both the piers and the cross beam were adorned with painted figures. Ceiling lights comprised four sculptured figures standing on a large illuminated sphere and holding lighted globes in their hands. Lighting was supplemented by jewel lamps of quaint design. The orchestra pit was deeply recessed below floor level.

At that time this was the only cinema in the town with a cafe, which was a lofty room to the left of the main stairway. It was finished in crimson, black, gold and blue with large, red-framed wall decorations and richly-coloured lights suspended from the ceiling. The decor of the ante-rooms and corridors was in harmony with that of the main building.

Scala entrance hall (1920's)

Scala cafe

Mr. J.S. Bramwell was in overall control of the reconstruction with artistic aspects of the re-design being provided by Mr. A. Auerbach, a talented Liverpool artist, with Mr. J. A. Milestone in charge of the building.

The final effect was successful and, after a postponement of one week, the cinema opened on the 25th April 1921 as the Scala Picture House. Those present included the new owners, Mr. W.W. Kelly the former owner, and the Mayor and Mayoress (Councillor Luke Lees and Miss Dorothy Lees) who declared the cinema open. After a rendition by Black's orchestra and an organ recital came the inaugural speeches when Mr. Kelly, who was clearly impressed with the transformation of the building, complimented management on their achievements. The formalities were followed by film shows. The first programme proper included 'Carnival' an all British production staring Matheson Lang, Hilda Bayley and Ivor Novello. Admission charges were 9d for the upper circle, 1/3 for the stalls and 2/- in the grand circle. A four piece orchestra provided musical interludes. The Scala was under the same management as the Claughton Picture House with Mrs. J. Sharp as general manageress and Mr. Alex Edwards as house manager and licensee. Implementation of plans for daily matinees at 3 o'clock with continuous performances from 6.30 to 10.30 p.m. (2.45 to 10.30 p.m. on Thursdays and Saturdays) had to be delayed because of the coal strike and limited supply of electricity and gas.

On the 5th of August 1929 the Scala became the first picture-house in Birkenhead to introduce talkies. The film chosen was *Sonny Boy* with young Davy Lee, Betty Bronson, Gertrude Olmstead, Edward E. Herton, Tom Dugan and J.T. Murray. It was an amusing tale in which an intended divorce brings about a romance. The performance was advertised as "one hundred percent talkie" and attracted such huge crowds that many were turned away from the box office in disappointment. Reporters were in no doubt "that this branch of cinematography will take on quickly" whilst others thought the gimmick would prove to be a fleeting curiosity.

In February 1930 the Scala was taken over by Associated British Cinemas and soon after it closed for two weeks extensive decoration. It re-opened on August Bank Holiday Monday with a performance of Monty Banks' *The Compulsory Husband*. The Scala finally closed its doors 6th of February 1937 with a showing of Bing Crosby in *Rhythm on the Range* and Joan Gardner in *Wings Over Africa*. This event proved to be rather an unusual affair in that the ex-Mayor, Mr. P.A. Allery, together with a party of officials formally performed a closing ceremony. He reminisced about the days when the building was the Theatre Royal under the ownership of the late Alderman W.W. Kelly, and he paid tribute to Mr. G.H. Baker, the current manager, for the standard of entertainment provided in more recent times and he wished him well in his new appointment in Hartlepool. Mr. Baker had been particularly successful in providing entertainment for old folks,

ex soldiers and even the blind. On the 31st October 1935, to celebrate the 71st birthday of the Theatre Royal Mr. Baker held a party with a number of guests all of whom were 71 years of age or older. At the time of closing it was claimed that the Scala was the only cinema on Merseyside using rear projection. Soon after closing the historic landmark was demolished to make way for another modern cinema, the Savoy.

Scala proscenium

OTHER TITLES FROM COUNTYVISE

Local History

Birkenhead Priory...Jean McInniss
Birkenhead Park...Jean McInniss
The Spire is Rising.. Dorothy Harden
The Search for Old Wirral...David Randall
Neston and Parkgate.. Jeffrey Pearson
Scotland Road..Terry Cooke
Helen Forrester Walk .... K. Rickard
Women at War .... Pat Ayres
Merseyside Moggies... R.M. Lewis
Dream Palaces..Harold Ackroyd
Forgotten Shores ....Maurice Hope
Cheshire Churches .... Roland W. Morant
Storm over the Mersey .... Beryl Wade
Memories of Heswall 1935 — 1985 .... Heswall W.E.A.

Local Railway Titles

Seventeen Stations to Dingle...John W. Gahan
The Line Beneath the Liners...John W. Gahan
Steel Wheels to Deeside...John W. Gahan
Seaport to Seaside ....John W. Gahan
Northern Rail Heritage ....K. Powell and G. Body
A Portrait of Wirral's Railways .... Roger Jermy

Local Shipping Titles

Sail on the Mersey...Michael Stammers
Ghost Ships on the Mersey ....K.J. Williams
The Liners of Liverpool – *Part I*...Derek Whale
The Liners of Liverpool – *Part II*..Derek Whale
The Liners of Liverpool – *Part III* ....Derek Whale
Hands off the Titanic...Monica O'Hara
Mr. Merch and other stories ....Ken Smith

Local Sport

The Liverpool Competition (Local Cricket)....................................P.N. Walker
Lottie Dod...Jeffrey Pearson

History with Humour

The One-Eyed City.. Rod Mackay
Hard Knocks... Rod Mackay
The Binmen are coming ....Louis Graham

Natural History

Birdwatching in Cheshire .... Eric Hardy

Other Titles

Speak through the Earthquake, Wind & Fire........................Graham A. Fisher
It's Me, O Lord... Members of Heswall Churches
Companion to the Fylde.. R.K. Davies
Country Walks on Merseyside.. David Parry
A-Z Cheshire Ghosts..Muriel Armand

OTHER TITLES FROM WIRRAL LIBRARIES

Birkenhead of Yesteryear..Carol Bidston
Della Robbia Pottery, Birkenhead..David Hillhouse
Hooton to West Kirby Branch Line .... Merseyside Railway History Group
The People's Garden.. Clifford Thornton
Up Our Lobby .... Bill Houldin
Wirral Visions ....Heather and Douglas Wilson